Current
CONTROVERSIES

▌Global Warming

Other Books in the Current Controversies Series

Alcoholism

Biodiversity

Drug Abuse

E-books

Family Violence

Gasoline

Media Ethics

Search and Seizure

Women in Politics

Global Warming

Debra A. Miller, Book Editor

GREENHAVEN PRESS
A part of Gale, Cengage Learning

Detroit • New York • San Francisco • New Haven, Conn • Waterville, Maine • London

Elizabeth Des Chenes, *Director, Publishing Solutions*

© 2013 Greenhaven Press, a part of Gale, Cengage Learning

Gale and Greenhaven Press are registered trademarks used herein under license.

For more information, contact:
Greenhaven Press
27500 Drake Rd.
Farmington Hills, MI 48331-3535
Or you can visit our Internet site at gale.cengage.com

For product information and technology assistance, contact us at

Gale Customer Support, 1-800-877-4253
For permission to use material from this text or product, submit all requests online at www.cengage.com/permissions

Further permissions questions can be emailed to permissionrequest@cengage.com

Articles in Greenhaven Press anthologies are often edited for length to meet page requirements. In addition, original titles of these works are changed to clearly present the main thesis and to explicitly indicate the author's opinion. Every effort is made to ensure that Greenhaven Press accurately reflects the original intent of the authors. Every effort has been made to trace the owners of copyrighted material.

Cover image © Ana de Sousa/Shutterstock.com.

LIBRARY OF CONGRESS CATALOGING-IN-PUBLICATION DATA

Global warming / Debra A. Miller, book editor.
    p. cm. -- (Current controversies)
  Includes bibliographical references and index.
  ISBN 978-0-7377-6229-7 (hardcover) -- ISBN 978-0-7377-6230-3 (pbk.)
  1. Global warming. I. Miller, Debra A. II. Series: Current controversies.
  QC981.8.G56G574414 2013
  363.738'74--dc23
                                                        2012031915

Printed in the United States of America
1 2 3 4 5   17 16 15 14 13

Contents

Foreword   **15**

Introduction   **18**

Chapter 1: Is Global Warming a Scientifically Proven Phenomenon?

Chapter Preface   **23**

Yes: Global Warming Is a Scientifically Proven Phenomenon

There Is Overwhelming Scientific   **26**
Consensus That Global Warming
Is Happening and Humans Are Causing It

Union of Concerned Scientists

Objections to taking action on climate change often point to scientific uncertainties about whether global warming is happening and whether it is caused by humans, but now there is broad agreement among scientists on both of these issues. Science societies, national science academies, researchers, and the Intergovernmental Panel on Climate Change (IPCC) have issued statements and publications attesting to this consensus.

The Fundamental Scientific Conclusions   **32**
About Global Warming Are Compelling

Peter Gleick and 187 Other Members of the US National Academy of Sciences

Science is never absolute, but the scientific evidence supporting global warming is as compelling as many other widely held theories, such as evolution, that are now accepted as fact. Nothing in the recent attacks on climate science changes the fundamental conclusions that the planet is warming due to human activities and causing rapid climate changes that threaten human beings and the natural ecosystems on which they depend.

Cooling the Warming Debate   **36**
Richard A. Muller

Skepticism about global warming once seemed appropriate, given the many variables and possible biases in the system of collecting and analyzing temperature records. However, research conducted by the Berkeley Earth Surface Temperature (BEST) Project has shown that climate researchers did accurate work, that global warming is real, and that it can no longer be questioned.

The CERN Study Does Not Disprove   40
Human-Caused Global Warming

Glenn Wright

Global warming skeptics have trumpeted a 2011 experiment by a group of scientists at CERN, the Swiss research institute, as proof that global warming is not caused by humans. However, this experiment was designed merely to test whether cosmic rays striking the earth's atmosphere contribute to cloud formation; it did not and was never intended to produce evidence about the effect of cosmic rays on climate.

New Research Suggests That   43
Global Warming Will Still Be Dangerous,
Though Not Extremely So

Andrew Freedman

Based on a 2011 study by researchers at Oregon State University, there may be less chance of extreme climate change than some climate models have predicted. Although some global warming skeptics suggest this means that climate concerns are overblown, climate scientists say this study is largely consistent with previous estimates and that global warming could still reach dangerous levels.

**No: Global Warming Is Not a Scientifically
Proven Phenomenon**

The BEST Study Did Not   48
Address Whether Humans Are
Causing Global Warming

Peter Ferrara

The BEST Project study, which was celebrated in the media as final proof of global warming, did not address the most important question—whether human activities are causing this warming. Also, the BEST study was limited to land temperature data and other evidence, such as data from satellites and weather balloons, that show no recent warming in the earth's atmosphere. Thus, the theory of human-made global warming remains unproven.

The BEST Study Hid the Critical   54
Fact That Global Warming Has Stopped
in Recent Years

David Rose

Although the BEST study was widely cited as final proof of global warming, one of the BEST researchers has claimed the project's own data shows instead that global warming has stopped and that there has been no increase in world temperatures since the late 1990s.

The CERN Study Demonstrates   60
That Nature, Not Humans, Controls the
Earth's Temperatures

Chriss W. Street

A 2011 climate study by the European Organization for Nuclear Research (CERN) found that cosmic rays from the sun can contribute to cloud formations and that the sun in this way controls temperatures on earth. This study thus undermines the theory that humans are causing global warming and proves there is no reason to cut greenhouse gas emissions.

The Science Shows There Will Be No   64
Apocalyptic Global Warming

Patrick Michaels

Years of satellite temperature measurements show that the Arctic is warming but the Antarctic is cooling and that this disparity will produce much more moderate global warming than the United Nations has forecast for this century. Global warming, therefore, is unlikely to be as catastrophic as many commentators have suggested.

Chapter 2: Are Global Warming Skeptics Motivated by Science?

Chapter Preface   68

Yes: Global Warming Skeptics Are Motivated by Science

The Number of Scientists Questioning   71
Global Warming Is Growing
    Claude Allegre et al.

A growing number of scientists and engineers do not believe that dramatic action is needed to stop global warming. One reason for doubt, for example, is that there has been no global warming for more than a decade. Even if global-warming forecasts are accurate, the best policy would be to allow for unimpeded economic growth for another fifty years.

Global-Warming Science Is Merely   77
a Working Hypothesis
    Gary M. Vasey

Human-caused global warming is merely a scientific hypothesis that should remain open to revision as new evidence is revealed. Although climate changes are occurring, the earth's climate has always changed, suggesting a complex group of natural causes rather than merely human-made carbon dioxide. Unfortunately, climate science has become highly politicized, with each side in the debate seeking to discredit the other rather than adhering to the scientific method.

Global-Warming Science Is New   84
and Untested
    Evan Sayet

Most people do not understand global warming science, but there are many good reasons to be skeptical about the claims put forth by global-warming alarmists. Some of these reasons are: that serious scientists question the theory, that climatology science is very new, and that climate models are based on data that cannot be verified. It is more likely that global warming is a cynical ruse designed to make money.

The Scientific and Policy Debate About   90
Global Warming Has Just Begun
    Karin McQuillan

Global warming became politicized early on, and the public has never been educated about how many scientists doubt the theory or the economic costs of reducing fossil fuel dependence. More and more scientists are challenging the so-called scientific consensus on global warming, however, so this may lead to more-truthful media coverage, better science, and a proper public debate about energy policy.

No: Global Warming Skeptics Are Not Motivated by Science

Scientists Who Deny Global Warming Rely on Falsehoods and Out-of-Date Research

Joe Romm

99

A 2012 *Wall Street Journal* article signed by sixteen scientists completely misrepresents climate science and contains only skeptics' talking points and falsehoods. For example, it is untrue that global warming has stopped; in fact, the last ten years were the hottest on record. If the world takes no action on global warming as these scientists suggest, there will most certainly be higher levels of warming and catastrophic impacts.

Global Warming Skeptics Are Motivated by Ideology, Not Science

Phil Plait

108

The Berkeley Earth Surface Temperature Project study was an independent study that confirmed what scientists have been saying for years—that the earth has warmed about a degree and that it has gotten especially hot during the last decade. Yet this new study is unlikely to convince global-warming deniers because they are concerned about ideology, not facts.

Skeptics Are Free-Market Fundamentalists Who Seek to Undermine Scientific Evidence of Global Warming

Naomi Oreskes and Erik M. Conway

113

As climate science and evidence of human involvement in climate change has strengthened, global-warming deniers have escalated their attacks on climate scientists, in some cases accusing them of criminal activity. This campaign is merely the latest version of a historic pattern by conservative free-market fundamentalists to deny and cause the public to doubt the seriousness of real environmental problems.

The Fossil Fuel Industry Is Funding   121
Global-Warming Denial
Bill McKibben

The virulent denial of global warming seen in the media
and in politics is clearly funded by the fossil fuel industry. This industry is making record profits right now, and
any efforts to reduce carbon emissions would destroy the
industry and its shareholders, so it funds denialism and
makes huge campaign contributions to prevent carbon
regulation.

Conservative Republicans Are in Denial   126
About Global-Warming Science
Michael Stafford

The evidence supporting human-caused global warming
is extensive and growing, and the scientific consensus is
that it will have a very negative effect on earth and life
on the planet unless action is taken soon. The radical
right wing of the Republican Party is in denial about climate change, however, so there is an urgent moral duty
for all people, especially conservatives, to speak out about
this issue.

Chapter 3: What Are the Predicted Impacts of Global Warming?

Chapter Preface   132

Many Climate Impacts Predicted by the   136
IPCC Are Already Happening
National Aeronautics and Space Administration

The Intergovernmental Panel on Climate Change (IPCC)
predicts that global temperatures will rise between 2.5
and 10 degrees Fahrenheit during the next one hundred
years and that this will have significant effects on the environment. Some of these effects are already being seen—
shrinking glaciers; shifting plant and animal ranges; loss
of sea, river, and lake ice; rises in sea levels; and more-
intense heat waves.

Snow and Ice Are Decreasing in the   140
Northern Hemisphere at Twice the Rate
Predicted by Climate Models
Pete Spotts

Climate scientists have predicted that warmer temperatures would decrease snow and ice in the Northern Hemisphere and that the lack of snow and ice in turn would produce greater global warming. A 2011 study confirmed that this feedback mechanism is at work but found that the snow and ice cover had decreased at twice the rate forecasted by climate models.

US Farmers Dodge the Impacts of Global Warming—at Least for Now, Stanford Researcher Says   144

Louis Bergeron

Although the United States so far has not experienced any agricultural production problems as a result of climate changes, a 2011 study by Stanford University found that most major crop-producing countries have suffered from reduced wheat and corn yields due to global warming. As temperatures continue to rise, the United States will also be affected.

Global Warming Is Increasing World Food Prices   148

Damian Carrington

New research has found that crop losses caused by global warming have hurt global food production and increased food prices by as much as 18.9 percent in recent decades. Long-term climate changes contributed to the decrease in food production, and short-term price hikes caused by extreme weather added to the problem.

Global Warming Will Likely Cause Serious Human Health Effects   152

Thilaka Ravi

Research shows that global warming may cause many different threats to health and human life. For example, malaria and other tropical diseases may spread; heat waves may cause heat strokes and death; malnutrition may increase due to agricultural stresses; and warmer temperatures may exacerbate air and water pollutions' effects on health.

Global Warming Poses a Grave Threat to Wildlife   156

E. Jean Brennan

Global warming is having significant effects on the natural world, and this is especially difficult for wildlife. In the Arctic, for example, polar bears are threatened by the loss of sea ice, while in the tropical oceans, coral reefs and invertebrate species are dying due to ocean warming and acidification. Indeed, declines in wildlife populations are occurring around the world as a result of a warming planet.

Global Warming Could Create Security Challenges for the US Military   162

Keith Randall

The climate changes brought by global warming will create a host of security challenges for the US military, according to a 2011 report issued by the Natural Resources Council. Melting sea ice in the Arctic, for example, opens that region to more transportation, energy exploration, and natural-resource exploitation—a scenario that could create conflicts among nations claiming those rights. The US military could also be called upon to respond to weather disasters around the globe caused by global warming.

Chapter 4: What Actions Should Be Taken to Address Global Warming?

Chapter Preface   167

National and Subnational Efforts, Rather than International Agreements, Are the Best Way to Address Global Warming   170

Harald Heubaum, as told to Responding to Climate Change

The Kyoto Protocol, an international treaty aimed at reducing global greenhouse gas emissions, which expires in 2012, is largely viewed as a failure. Even so, international efforts such as the Kyoto Protocol should not be scrapped but should be combined with national and subnational efforts—such as fuel efficiency standards and renewable portfolio standards—as the best way to address global warming.

The World Should End Fossil Fuel Subsidies to Achieve Emission Reductions   175

Matthew Yglesias

A 2012 report by the International Energy Agency found that eliminating fossil fuel subsidies would go halfway toward reducing enough greenhouse gas emissions to prevent global warming from rising above two degrees Celsius—considered the safe level. The biggest subsidies are in oil-producing countries, but the United States and developing countries like China, India, and Indonesia also have large subsidies.

Efforts to Slow Global Warming   179
Should Focus on Methane and Soot
Instead of Carbon Dioxide
R.P. Siegel

Global-warming efforts to date have focused mostly on reducing carbon dioxide emissions, but NASA scientists say it might be more effective initially to reduce methane and soot. These pollutants could significantly reduce warming in the near term using existing technologies, such as capturing methane from landfills and modifying agricultural practices.

Governments Must Support New Green   182
Energy Technologies More Quickly
Institution of Mechanical Engineers

Technologies to reduce global warming—such as wind, wave, solar, and others—already have been proven, but their development is lagging due to the absence of government support. Governments must commit to reducing emissions by adopting and funding green policies that promote these technologies and improve energy efficiency on a global scale.

Geoengineering Research Should Be   186
Pursued as a Solution to Global Warming
Dan Vergano

Failed efforts to reduce greenhouse gas emissions are leading to a push for research into geoengineering—large-scale engineering projects to reduce sunlight or carbon dioxide in the atmosphere as a way to slow global warming. Proponents say this research should begin in earnest so that it is available when needed in the future, but critics note that this strategy poses risks to the environment and may have other unforeseen consequences.

The World Should Not Waste Resources   193
on Fighting Global Warming
Richard S. Lindzen

The earth's climate is always in flux, and the contribution of carbon dioxide to the atmosphere, by itself, does not create much global warming. Despite the alarmist predictions about climate change, the scientific evidence suggests that human-caused global warming has been greatly exaggerated, so it is important for leaders to resist the calls for massive carbon taxation schemes to regulate greenhouse gases.

Only Immediate Action Will Keep Global Warming Below Dangerous Levels

Richard A. Kerr

A new 2011 study examined various scenarios for cutting greenhouse gas emissions and found that only immediate and dramatic actions could keep global warming below two degrees Celsius—considered to be a safe level. The only strategies that have a chance of success call for the widespread adoption of new types of energy—such as biofuels and energy systems that remove carbon dioxide from the atmosphere.

200

Organizations to Contact   202

Bibliography   207

Index   213

Foreword

By definition, controversies are "discussions of questions in which opposing opinions clash" (*Webster's Twentieth Century Dictionary Unabridged*). Few would deny that controversies are a pervasive part of the human condition and exist on virtually every level of human enterprise. Controversies transpire between individuals and among groups, within nations and between nations. Controversies supply the grist necessary for progress by providing challenges and challengers to the status quo. They also create atmospheres where strife and warfare can flourish. A world without controversies would be a peaceful world; but it also would be, by and large, static and prosaic.

The Series' Purpose

The purpose of the Current Controversies series is to explore many of the social, political, and economic controversies dominating the national and international scenes today. Titles selected for inclusion in the series are highly focused and specific. For example, from the larger category of criminal justice, Current Controversies deals with specific topics such as police brutality, gun control, white collar crime, and others. The debates in Current Controversies also are presented in a useful, timeless fashion. Articles and book excerpts included in each title are selected if they contribute valuable, long-range ideas to the overall debate. And wherever possible, current information is enhanced with historical documents and other relevant materials. Thus, while individual titles are current in focus, every effort is made to ensure that they will not become quickly outdated. Books in the Current Controversies series will remain important resources for librarians, teachers, and students for many years.

In addition to keeping the titles focused and specific, great care is taken in the editorial format of each book in the series. Book introductions and chapter prefaces are offered to provide background material for readers. Chapters are organized around several key questions that are answered with diverse opinions representing all points on the political spectrum. Materials in each chapter include opinions in which authors clearly disagree as well as alternative opinions in which authors may agree on a broader issue but disagree on the possible solutions. In this way, the content of each volume in Current Controversies mirrors the mosaic of opinions encountered in society. Readers will quickly realize that there are many viable answers to these complex issues. By questioning each author's conclusions, students and casual readers can begin to develop the critical thinking skills so important to evaluating opinionated material.

Current Controversies is also ideal for controlled research. Each anthology in the series is composed of primary sources taken from a wide gamut of informational categories including periodicals, newspapers, books, US and foreign government documents, and the publications of private and public organizations. Readers will find factual support for reports, debates, and research papers covering all areas of important issues. In addition, an annotated table of contents, an index, a book and periodical bibliography, and a list of organizations to contact are included in each book to expedite further research.

Perhaps more than ever before in history, people are confronted with diverse and contradictory information. During the Persian Gulf War, for example, the public was not only treated to minute-to-minute coverage of the war, it was also inundated with critiques of the coverage and countless analyses of the factors motivating US involvement. Being able to sort through the plethora of opinions accompanying today's major issues, and to draw one's own conclusions, can be a complicated and frustrating struggle. It is the editors' hope that Current Controversies will help readers with this struggle.

Introduction

"Unlike prehistoric climate variations, today's warming trend . . . is related to human activities, and unless remedial action is taken in the near future, the trend is expected to bring significant changes to the earth's climate that will be detrimental to all living things."

Over the 4.5 billion years that the earth has existed, its climate has constantly been in flux, sometimes dominated by ice ages where glaciers covered much of the planet and other times experiencing warming trends where ice retreated to the North and South Poles. For many thousands of years, the planet has been enjoying a long interglacial warm period, but the current global warming and climate change debate involves a much more recent phenomenon—a rapid rise in average global temperatures over the last century that many scientists attribute to the release of carbon dioxide and other so-called greenhouse gases, largely as a result of the burning of fossil fuels such as coal, oil, and natural gas. Unlike prehistoric climate variations, therefore, today's warming trend, these scientists believe, is related to human activities, and unless remedial action is taken in the near future, the trend is expected to bring significant changes to the earth's climate that will be detrimental to all living things.

Humans have known about global warming since the 1800s. The first scientist to propose that humans could affect the global climate was Svante Arrhenius, a Swede who in 1896 speculated that the burning of fossil fuels such as coal could increase the concentration of carbon dioxide in the atmosphere and add to the earth's natural greenhouse effect—the process in which heat is trapped by atmospheric gases, such as carbon dioxide, methane, water vapor, and ozone. Systematic research into global warming, however, did not begin until the mid-1900s, when scientists began studying global temperature patterns and other information related to weather and climate. Scientific attention to global warming initially was muted, however, because scientists instead discovered a global cooling deviation that began in the 1940s and caused many people to doubt the global-warming theory.

In the 1980s, many scientists warned of a looming environmental crisis involving a hole in the ozone layer—part of the earth's stratosphere that prevents damaging ultraviolet sunlight from hitting the planet. These scientists concluded that this climate emergency was caused by humans' use of products such as refrigerants and aerosol sprays containing chlorofluorocarbons (CFCs). The world's governments responded in 1987 with the Montreal Protocol, a highly successful international agreement that soon halted the production of CFCs around the globe. The elimination of CFCs, along with legislation that reduced other industrial air pollutants, most scientists believe, ended the temporary cooling trend and allowed global warming to resume. Scientific concerns thus shifted back to global warming.

As it did after the discovery of the ozone crisis, the international community responded to scientific warnings about global warming. The United Nations established the Intergovernmental Panel on Climate Change (IPCC) in 1988, charging it with reviewing and reporting on the scientific evidence of global warming and climate change. The first IPCC report on global warming was issued in 1990, but there was a lack of scientific consensus at that point on just how much increased greenhouse effect was being caused by humans, as opposed to natural processes. Nevertheless, most scientists remained concerned about the possibility of significant climate change induced by gas emissions, and they convinced world leaders to meet in 1992 in Rio de Janeiro, Brazil, for the first Earth Summit, where they agreed to a treaty—the United Nations Framework Convention on Climate Change (UNFCCC or FCCC)—that aimed at stabilizing greenhouse gas emissions. Media coverage of global warming spiked a few years later, when the IPCC released its 1995 report, which for the first time found that global warming was a reality and was likely caused by human activities. Two years later, at a 1997 international climate conference held in Kyoto, Japan, delegates from many countries adopted the Kyoto Protocol—an international agreement designed to enforce the UNFCCC through mandatory cuts in greenhouse gas emissions.

In 2001, the IPCC released its third report, concluding that the world was most definitely warming and that most of this warming was probably caused by human activity. Furthermore, the report predicted that the warming would continue and unless action was taken to limit emissions, could result in potentially severe consequences. Although the IPCC report embodied the consensus opinion of most of the world's preeminent geoscientists, its findings were increasingly challenged by global warming skeptics, who charged that global warming was a hoax and that humans cannot have such a profound effect on climate. Critics charged that many of the global warming skeptics and media campaigns received funding from oil industry companies like Exxon-Mobil. As later IPCC reports reached stronger and stronger conclusions about global warming, the voices doubting climate science grew stronger as well. Polls of Americans' attitudes about global warming showed that anti-global-warming efforts had worked and that people increasingly doubted that global warming was an issue that required government action.

Meanwhile, although the Kyoto Protocol did cause ratifying countries to reduce their carbon emissions, the treaty failed to make significant progress on reducing global greenhouse gas emissions. One reason was that it was focused solely on industrialized nations and failed to set emissions limits on rapidly developing countries, such as China and India, whose emissions were increasing along with their economic development. Another reason was that the United States, the world's largest consumer of energy and emitter of greenhouse gases, refused to ratify the protocol, mainly because it did not also cover developing countries. While many European nations struggled to reduce their greenhouse emissions to meet mandatory Kyoto targets, the United States government acceded to the interests of industrial groups that opposed any type of carbon regulation. Meanwhile, many of the countries that did ratify Kyoto found it very difficult to reduce their emissions, largely because of the economic costs of cutting back on fossil fuels when no equally cheap alternative energy was available. The Kyoto Protocol is due to expire at the end of 2012, and observers say it is unlikely to be replaced by a similar treaty.

The issue of global warming thus remains a controversial one today, with dueling opinions in the media over the existence of human-caused climate changes and no clear path forward for responding to this potentially catastrophic environmental threat. The authors of the viewpoints in *Current Controversies: Global Warming* offer various perspectives on this topic, including whether global warming is a scientifically proven phenomenon, whether global warming skeptics base their objections on science, what the predicted impacts of climate change are, and what actions should be taken to address global warming.

CHAPTER 1

Is Global Warming a Scientifically Proven Phenomenon?

Chapter Preface

The Intergovernmental Panel on Climate Change (IPCC) is a scientific body created by the United Nations in 1988 and charged with collecting, synthesizing, and reporting all the best scientific evidence on global warming and the climate changes caused by warmer temperatures. Over the years, the IPCC has released four separate reports, each of which assessed the then-current knowledge about global warming and made predictions about future warming and expected impacts. The IPCC's most recent assessment report—Climate Change 2007—included input from more than twelve hundred authors and twenty-five hundred expert scientific reviewers from over 130 countries, and contained the strongest warning yet about climate change.

The highlight of the 2007 report was its conclusion that the evidence of the warming of our climate is now "unequivocal."[1] In addition, the report concluded that most of the increase in globally averaged temperatures since the mid-twentieth century is "very likely"[2] due to human activities, such as the burning of fossil fuels like coal, oil, and natural gas. The IPCC defines *very likely* to mean 90 percent certainty. According to the IPCC, global greenhouse gas (GHG) emissions have increased at an unprecedented rate since preindustrial times—including an increase of 70 percent between 1970 and 2004. The current atmospheric concentration of two main greenhouse gases, carbon dioxide and methane, the report said, far exceeds what had been the natural levels of these gases over the last 650,000 years.

The impacts of global warming are already being felt, according to the IPCC. The 2007 report, for example, noted that eleven of the last twelve years rank among the hottest years on record since global temperature measurements began in 1850. These temperature changes, the report says, have brought fewer cold days and frost and more frequent hot days and heat waves. In addition, the world has seen increasingly severe weather in the form of bigger storms that bring heavy precipitation, more intense hurricanes, and more droughts and expanding deserts. Global warming has also been responsible for widespread melting of snow and ice, decreasing the size of mountain glaciers and snow cover worldwide and causing Arctic sea ice to shrink by more than 20 percent since 1978. Meanwhile, the IPCC explains that the world's oceans have been absorbing much of the heat from global warming, causing expansion; this, together with melting glaciers and snowpacks, are causing average sea levels to slowly rise.

The 2007 report explained that predictions of future climate change depend on the level of future greenhouse gas emissions. The report, therefore, made predictions based on six different scenarios—from the most optimistic to the most pessimistic (although all scenarios assumed that the world population will level off around mid-century). The most optimistic scenario, for example, would result in relatively slight temperature increases, but it assumes a rapid change toward a service and information economy and a shift away from fossil fuels toward clean and resource-efficient technologies. The most pessimistic scenario, on the other hand, entails much hotter temperatures and assumes that today's rapid economic growth would continue without significant change, using mostly fossil-fuel-based energy production and consumption. The temperature increases projected by the report are between 2 and 11.5 degrees Fahrenheit (1.1 to 6.4 degrees Celsius) by the end of the century. The report warns, however, that even if the world acted immediately to reduce emissions from cars, power plants, land use, and other sources, there will be continued warming because past emissions will stay in the atmosphere for at least decades.

The IPCC's direst warning is that if humans make no effort to reduce greenhouse gas emissions, the global-warming process will continue, bringing possibly irreversible consequences for the planet. According to the 2007 report, within just a few decades these consequences could include the loss of up to 30 percent of animal and plant species, large-scale degradation of world fisheries, and damage to water and land resources and ecosystems—all of which could threaten human health and jeopardize global food production. Continued warming could also cause staggering economic losses; British economist Nicholas Stern has estimated that the weather impacts of global warming could reduce global economic output by 20 percent.

Recent research suggests that global-warming impacts may be even worse than these 2007 IPCC projections. Studies have found, for example, that Arctic ice is melting much faster than the IPCC's worst-case scenario predictions and may completely disappear within five years. The absence of Arctic ice could, in turn, speed up other warming effects, creating even more warming than predicted. On the other hand, other studies of the planet's sensitivity to carbon dioxide levels during prehistoric ice ages suggest that some of the most extreme IPCC predictions of climate change may be less likely than once believed. There is still some uncertainty about global warming within the scientific community, therefore, because climate science is always evolving. The authors of the viewpoints in this chapter tackle the most fundamental of the issues in the global-warming debate—whether global warming has been scientifically proven to exist.

Notes

1. Intergovernmental Panel on Climate Change, "Climate Change 2007: Synthesis Report, Summary for Policymakers," November 2007, p. 2. www.ipcc.ch/pdf/assessment-re port/ar4/syr/ar4_syr_spm.pdf.
2. Intergovernmental Panel on Climate Change, "Climate Change 2007," p. 5.

There Is Overwhelming Scientific Consensus That Global Warming Is Happening and Humans Are Causing It

Union of Concerned Scientists

The Union of Concerned Scientists is a science-based nonprofit research and policy organization that works for a healthy environment and a safer world.

Scientific societies and scientists have released statements and studies showing the growing consensus on climate change science. A common objection to taking action to reduce our heat-trapping emissions has been uncertainty within the scientific community on whether or not global warming is happening and if it is caused by humans. However, there is now an overwhelming scientific consensus that global warming is indeed happening and humans are contributing to it. Below [is a list of] ... documents and statements attesting to this consensus.

• Statement on climate change from 18 scientific associations:

"Observations throughout the world make it clear that climate change is occurring, and rigorous scientific research demonstrates that the greenhouse gases emitted by human activities are the primary driver." (October 2009)

• American Meteorological Society: Climate Change: An Information Statement of the American Meteorological Society:

"Indeed, strong observational evidence and results from modeling studies indicate that, at least over the last 50 years, human activities are a major contributor to climate change." (February 2007)

• American Physical Society: Statement on Climate Change:

"The evidence is incontrovertible: Global warming is occurring. If no mitigating actions are taken, significant disruptions in the Earth's physical and ecological systems, social systems, security and human health are likely to occur. We must reduce emissions of greenhouse gases beginning now." (November 2007)

The scientific evidence is clear: global climate change caused by human activities is occurring now, and it is a growing threat to society.

• American Geophysical Union: Human Impacts on Climate:

"The Earth's climate is now clearly out of balance and is warming. Many components of the climate system—including the temperatures of the atmosphere, land and ocean, the extent of sea ice and mountain glaciers, the sea level, the distribution of precipitation, and the length of seasons—are now changing at rates and in patterns that are not natural and are best explained by the increased atmospheric abundances of greenhouse gases and aerosols generated by human activity during the 20th century." (Adopted December 2003, Revised and Reaffirmed December 2007)

• American Association for the Advancement of Science: AAAS Board Statement on Climate Change:

"The scientific evidence is clear: global climate change caused by human activities is occurring now, and it is a growing threat to society." (December 2006)

• Geological Society of America: Global Climate Change:

"The Geological Society of America (GSA) supports the scientific conclusions that Earth's climate is changing; the climate changes are due in part to human activities; and the probable consequences of the climate changes will be significant and blind to geopolitical boundaries." (October 2006)

• American Chemical Society: Statement on Global Climate Change:

"There is now general agreement among scientific experts that the recent warming trend is real (and particularly strong within the past 20 years), that most of the observed warming is likely due to increased atmospheric greenhouse gas concentrations, and that climate change could have serious adverse effects by the end of this century." (July 2004)

National Science Academies

• U.S. National Academy of Sciences: Understanding and Responding to Climate Change:

"The scientific understanding of climate change is now sufficiently clear to justify taking steps to reduce the amount of greenhouse gases in the atmosphere." (2005)

• International academies: Joint science academies' statement: Global response to climate change:

"Climate change is real. There will always be uncertainty in understanding a system as complex as the world's climate. However there is now strong evidence that significant global warming is occurring." (2005, 11 national academies of science)

• International academies: The Science of Climate Change:

"Despite increasing consensus on the science underpinning predictions of global climate change, doubts have been expressed recently about the need to mitigate the risks posed by global climate change. We do not consider such doubts justified." (2001, 16 national academies of science)

• National Research Council of the National Academies, America's Climate Choices: Advancing the Science of Climate Change:

"Most of the recent warming can be attributed to fossil fuel burning and other human activities that release carbon dioxide and other heat-trapping greenhouse gases into the atmosphere." (2010)

• U.S. Climate Change Research Program, Global Climate Change Impacts in the United States:

"Global warming is unequivocal and primarily human-induced. Global temperature has increased over the past 50 years. This observed increase is due primarily to human-induced emissions of heat-trapping gases." (2009)

• Examining the Scientific Consensus on Climate Change, Peter T. Doran and Maggie Kendall Zimmerman:

"It seems that the debate on the authenticity of global warming and the role played by human activity is largely non-existent among those who understand the nuances and scientific basis of long-term climate processes."

Doran surveyed 10,257 Earth scientists. Thirty percent responded to the survey which asked: 1. When compared with pre-1800s levels, do you think that mean global temperatures have generally risen, fallen, or remained relatively constant? and 2. Do you think human activity is a significant contributing factor in changing mean global temperatures?

Peer-Reviewed Journals

• Naomi Oreskes, Beyond the Ivory Tower: The Scientific Consensus on Climate Change:

"Oreskes analyzed 928 abstracts published in refereed scientific journals between 1993 and 2003 and listed in the ISI [Institute for Scientific Information] database with the keywords 'climate change.' ... Of all the papers, 75 percent either explicitly or implicitly accepted the consensus view that global warming is happening and humans are contributing to it; 25

percent dealt with methods or ancient climates, taking no position on current anthropogenic [human-caused] climate change. Remarkably, none of the papers disagreed with the consensus position."

• Climate Change 2007: The Physical Science Basis, IPCC. Contribution of Working Group I to the Fourth Assessment Report of the Intergovernmental Panel on Climate Change [Solomon, S., D. Qin, M. Manning, Z. Chen, M. Marquis, K.B. Averyt, M. Tignor and H.L. Miller,eds.]. Cambridge University Press, Cambridge, United Kingdom and New York, NY, USA:

We want to assure you that the science is strong and that there is nothing abstract about the risks facing our Nation.

"Warming of the climate system is unequivocal, as is now evident from observations of increases in global average air and ocean temperatures, widespread melting of snow and ice, and rising global average sea level."

"Most of the observed increase in global average temperatures since the mid-20th century is very likely due to the observed increase in anthropogenic greenhouse gas concentrations."

IPCC defines "very likely" as greater than 90% probability of occurrence. (2007)

Sign-on Statements

• The Importance of Science in Addressing Climate Change: Scientists' letter to the U.S. Congress. Statement signed by 18 scientists:

"We want to assure you that the science is strong and that there is nothing abstract about the risks facing our Nation." (2011)

• Climate Change and the Integrity of Science Signed by 255 members of the National Academy of Sciences:

"... For a problem as potentially catastrophic as climate change, taking no action poses a dangerous risk for our planet.... The planet is warming due to increased concentrations of heat-trapping gases in our atmosphere.... Most of the increase in the concentration of these gases over the last century is due to human activities, especially the burning of fossil fuels and deforestation." (2010)

• U.S. Scientists and Economists' Call for Swift and Deep Cuts in Greenhouse Gas Emissions:

"We call on our nation's leaders to swiftly establish and implement policies to bring about deep reductions in heat-trapping emissions. The strength of the science on climate change compels us to warn the nation about the growing risk of irreversible consequences as global average temperatures continue to increase over pre-industrial levels (i.e. prior to 1860). As temperatures rise further, the scope and severity of global warming impacts will continue to accelerate." (2008)

• Increase Your Leadership on Global Warming: A Letter from California Scientists:

"If emissions continue unabated, the serious consequences of a changing climate for California are likely to include a striking increase in extreme heat and heat-related mortality, significant reductions in Sierra snowpack with severe impacts on water supply, mounting challenges to agricultural production, and sea-level rise leading to more widespread erosion of California's beaches and coastline." (2005)

The Fundamental Scientific Conclusions About Global Warming Are Compelling

Peter Gleick and 187 Other Members of the US National Academy of Sciences

Peter Gleick and the other 187 signatories are distinguished scholars, scientists, and engineers who are members of the US National Academy of Sciences (NAS), a private, nonprofit organization created by President Abraham Lincoln in 1863 to provide independent advice to the government on matters of science and technology.

We are deeply disturbed by the recent escalation of political assaults on scientists in general and on climate scientists in particular. All citizens should understand some basic scientific facts. There is always some uncertainty associated with scientific conclusions; science never absolutely proves anything. When someone says that society should wait until scientists are absolutely certain before taking any action, it is the same as saying society should never take action. For a problem as potentially catastrophic as climate change, taking no action poses a dangerous risk for our planet.

Scientific conclusions derive from an understanding of basic laws supported by laboratory experiments, observations of nature, and mathematical and computer modeling. Like all human beings, scientists make mistakes, but the scientific process is designed to find and correct them. This process is inherently adversarial—scientists build reputations and gain recognition not only for supporting conventional wisdom, but even more so for demonstrating that the scientific consensus is wrong and that there is a better explanation. That's what Galileo [Galilei], [Louis] Pasteur, [Charles] Darwin, and [Albert] Einstein did. But when some conclusions have been thoroughly and deeply tested, questioned, and examined, they gain the status of "well-established theories" and are often spoken of as "facts."

There is nothing remotely identified in the recent events that changes the fundamental conclusions about climate change.

For instance, there is compelling scientific evidence that our planet is about 4.5 billion years old (the theory of the origin of Earth), that our universe was born from a single event about 14 billion years ago (the Big Bang theory), and that today's organisms evolved from ones living in the past (the theory of evolution). Even as these are overwhelmingly accepted by the scientific community, fame still awaits anyone who could show these theories to be wrong. Climate change now falls into this category: There is compelling, comprehensive, and consistent objective evidence that humans are changing the climate in ways that threaten our societies and the ecosystems on which we depend.

Many recent assaults on climate science and, more disturbingly, on climate scientists by climate change deniers are typically driven by special interests or dogma, not by an honest effort to provide an alternative theory that credibly satisfies the evidence. The Intergovernmental Panel on Climate Change (IPCC) and other scientific assessments of climate change, which involve thousands of scientists producing massive and comprehensive reports, have, quite expectedly and normally, made some mistakes. When errors are pointed out, they are corrected. But there is nothing remotely identified in the recent events that changes the fundamental conclusions about climate change:

(i) The planet is warming due to increased concentrations of heat-trapping gases in our atmosphere. A snowy winter in Washington does not alter this fact.

(ii) Most of the increase in the concentration of these gases over the last century is due to human activities, especially the burning of fossil fuels and deforestation.

(iii) Natural causes always play a role in changing Earth's climate, but are now being overwhelmed by human-induced changes.

(iv) Warming the planet will cause many other climatic patterns to change at speeds unprecedented in modern times, including increasing rates of sea-level rise and alterations in the hydrologic cycle. Rising concentrations of carbon dioxide are making the oceans more acidic.

(v) The combination of these complex climate changes threatens coastal communities and cities, our food and water supplies, marine and freshwater ecosystems, forests, high mountain environments, and far more.

Immediate Action Needed

Much more can be, and has been, said by the world's scientific societies, national academies, and individuals, but these conclusions should be enough to indicate why scientists are concerned about what future generations will face from business-as-usual practices. We urge our policy-makers and the public to move forward immediately to address the causes of climate change, including the unrestrained burning of fossil fuels.

We also call for an end to McCarthy-like [US senator Joseph McCarthy accused people of being Communists in the 1950s, usually without evidence] threats of criminal prosecution against our colleagues based on innuendo and guilt by association, the harassment of scientists by politicians seeking distractions to avoid taking action, and the outright lies being spread about them. Society has two choices: We can ignore the science and hide our heads in the sand and hope we are lucky, or we can act in the public interest to reduce the threat of global climate change quickly and substantively. The good news is that smart and effective actions are possible. But delay must not be an option.

Cooling the Warming Debate

Richard A. Muller

Richard A. Muller is a professor of physics at the University of California, Berkeley. He founded and directs the Berkeley Earth Surface Temperature (BEST) Project to research and resolve current criticism of previous analyses of the surface temperature record used to determine the extent of global warming.

Are you a global warming skeptic? There are plenty of good reasons why you might be.

As many as 757 stations in the United States recorded net surface-temperature cooling over the past century. Many are concentrated in the southeast, where some people attribute tornadoes and hurricanes to warming.

The temperature-station quality is largely awful. The most important stations in the U.S. are included in the Department of Energy's Historical Climatology Network. A careful survey of these stations by a team led by meteorologist Anthony Watts showed that 70% of these stations have such poor siting that, by the U.S. government's own measure, they result in temperature uncertainties of between two and five degrees Celsius or more. We do not know how much worse are the stations in the developing world.

Using data from all these poor stations, the U.N.'s Intergovernmental Panel on Climate Change [IPCC] estimates an average global 0.64°C temperature rise in the past 50 years, "most" of which the IPCC says is due to humans. Yet the margin of error for the stations is at least three times larger than the estimated warming.

We know that cities show anomalous warming, caused by energy use and building materials; asphalt, for instance, absorbs more sunlight than do trees. Tokyo's temperature rose about 2°C in the last 50 years. Could that rise, and increases in other urban areas, have been unreasonably included in the global estimates? That warming may be real, but it has nothing to do with the greenhouse effect and can't be addressed by carbon dioxide reduction.

[Data] adjustments often result in corrections of several tenths of one degree Celsius, significant fractions of the warming attributed to humans.

Moreover, the three major temperature analysis groups (the U.S.'s NASA and National Oceanic and Atmospheric Administration, and the U.K.'s Met Office and Climatic Research Unit) analyze only a small fraction of the available data, primarily from stations that have long records. There's a logic to that practice, but it could lead to selection bias. For instance, older stations were often built outside of cities but today are surrounded by buildings. These groups today use data from about 2,000 stations, down from roughly 6,000 in 1970, raising even more questions about their selections.

On top of that, stations have moved, instruments have changed and local environments have evolved. Analysis groups try to compensate for all this by homogenizing the data, though there are plenty of arguments to be had over how best to homogenize long-running data taken from around the world in varying conditions. These adjustments often result in corrections of several tenths of one degree Celsius, significant fractions of the warming attributed to humans.

And that's just the surface-temperature record. What about the rest? The number of named hurricanes has been on the rise for years, but that's in part a result of better detection technologies (satellites and buoys) that find storms in remote regions. The number of hurricanes hitting the U.S., even more intense Category 4 and 5 storms, has been gradually decreasing since 1850. The number of detected tornadoes has been increasing, possibly because radar technology has improved, but the number that touch down and cause damage has been decreasing. Meanwhile, the short-term variability in U.S. surface temperatures has been decreasing since 1800, suggesting a more stable climate.

Without good answers to all these complaints, global-warming skepticism seems sensible. But now let me explain why you should not be a skeptic, at least not any longer.

The BEST Study

Over the last two years, the Berkeley Earth Surface Temperature [BEST] Project has looked deeply at all the issues raised above. I chaired our group, which just submitted four detailed papers on our results to peer-reviewed journals. We have now posted these papers online at *www.BerkeleyEarth.org* to solicit even more scrutiny.

Our work covers only land temperature—not the oceans—but that's where warming appears to be the greatest. Robert Rohde, our chief scientist, obtained more than 1.6 billion measurements from more than 39,000 temperature stations around the world. Many of the records were short in duration, and to use them Mr. Rohde and a team of esteemed scientists and statisticians developed a new analytical approach that let us incorporate fragments of records. By using data from virtually all the available stations, we avoided data-selection bias. Rather than try to correct for the discontinuities in the records, we simply sliced the records where the data cut off, thereby creating two records from one.

We discovered that about one-third of the world's temperature stations have recorded cooling temperatures, and about two-thirds have recorded warming. The two-to-one ratio reflects global warming. The changes at the locations that showed warming were typically between 1–2°C, much greater than the IPCC's average of 0.64°C.

Global warming is real. Perhaps our results will help cool this portion of the climate debate.

To study urban-heating bias in temperature records, we used satellite determinations that subdivided the world into urban and rural areas. We then conducted a temperature analysis based solely on "very rural" locations, distant from urban ones. The result showed a temperature increase similar to that found by other groups. Only 0.5% of the globe is urbanized, so it makes sense that even a 2°C rise in urban regions would contribute negligibly to the global average.

What about poor station quality? Again, our statistical methods allowed us to analyze the U.S. temperature record separately for stations with good or acceptable rankings, and those with poor rankings (the U.S. is the only place in the world that ranks its temperature stations). Remarkably, the poorly ranked stations showed no greater temperature increases than the better ones. The most likely explanation is that while low-quality stations may give incorrect absolute temperatures, they still accurately track temperature changes.

When we began our study, we felt that skeptics had raised legitimate issues, and we didn't know what we'd find. Our results turned out to be close to those published by prior groups. We think that means that those groups had truly been very careful in their work, despite their inability to convince some skeptics of that. They managed to avoid bias in their data selection, homogenization and other corrections.

Global warming is real. Perhaps our results will help cool this portion of the climate debate. How much of the warming is due to humans and what will be the likely effects? We made no independent assessment of that.

The CERN Study Does Not Disprove Human-Caused Global Warming

Glenn Wright

Glenn Wright is a national political writer for Examiner.com, a media company based in Denver, Colorado, that operates a network of websites offering local news.

The problem with science is that few people can do it, or really understand its implications, but everybody gets to interpret scientific studies as they see fit.

Often they see fit to be utterly misleading.

Descriptions like "convincing evidence" (usually supporting a political, not a scientific, agenda) are often nothing more than slogans attached by political partisans to misreadings of the scientific data, or even of what scientists themselves have clearly said about their understanding of it.

For example, recently a group of CERN [European Organization for Nuclear Research] scientists completed an experiment (with the acronym CLOUD) designed to test the possibility that cosmic rays hitting the Earth's atmosphere may contribute to cloud formation. The test was never intended to conclusively demonstrate such a phenomenon was actually occurring—for one thing the test was conducted inside CERN's atmosphere chamber, a closed and highly controlled environment—and not in the much more complex atmosphere of Earth.

When the test provided results that indicated that some change was happening when CERN's simulated atmosphere was bombarded with simulated cosmic rays, the scientists in charge recorded this result, and called it an important first step in their research.

However, Jasper Kirkby, the lead scientist on the project, whose work is often pointed to by climate-change skeptics as "proof" that any climate change taking place is not manmade, said the following regarding his experiment, noting that the level of change in chemistry found in the experiment was insufficient to support a cloud formation process:

"At the moment, [the experiment] actually says nothing about a possible cosmic-ray effect on clouds and climate."

This "nothing" was magically transformed by climate-change skeptics and deniers into the aforementioned "convincing evidence".

[CERN's lead scientist] specifically denied the CERN cloud formation experiment concluded anything about the cause of climate change.

For example, Lawrence Solomon, a climate-change skeptic writing for the *Financial Post*, claimed:

"The science is now all-but-settled on global warming, convincing new evidence demonstrates ... [t]he new findings point to cosmic rays and the sun—not human activities—as the dominant controller of climate on Earth."

Solomon noted that Jasper Kirkby had declared the matter all but decided over a decade ago, even though that isn't what Kirkby actually said at all, and as noted above he specifically denied the CERN cloud formation experiment concluded anything about the cause of climate change.

Solomon claims any such denial on Kirkby's part comes from a conspiracy of pressure placed upon him by CERN and other political and ideological interests who wish to support an anthropogenic model of global warming.

In fact, the science the CERN experiment was intended to give some insight concerning, is some of the most complex scientific work there is. The CLOUD research was never intended to be conclusive concerning a political agenda, but to provide a better understanding—to scientists—of what additional elements might be in play in atmospheric chemistry. That may, eventually, give scientists a better understanding of the cumulative effects of different contributors to climate change.

But, in no way does the CERN experiment point to the conclusion claimed about it by so many commentators and bloggers. In fact, the CLOUD press release plainly says:

"it is premature to conclude that cosmic rays have significant influence on climate."

New Research Suggests That Global Warming Will Still Be Dangerous, Though Not Extremely So

Andrew Freedman

Andrew Freedman is an environmental journalist and blogger for the Capital Weather Gang, *a blog at the website of the* Washington Post.

New research takes some of the most dire global warming projections off the table. A study published last week [November 27, 2011,] in the journal *Science* concludes that the more extreme climate change scenarios, which involve temperature increases of up to 10°F are implausible. Instead, the study finds, we are likely in the midst of a more manageable, but still potentially dangerous, shift in the planet's climate.

In fact, this study's projections still warm the planet to the highest levels in human history.

According to the study, if atmospheric concentrations of carbon dioxide (CO_2), the most important global warming gas, were to double, the global average surface temperature would increase by between 3 to 4.7°F, with a median value of 4.1°F (or 1.7 to 2.6°C, with a median value of 2.3°C). This is a narrower range, with a lower upper estimate, than other studies have concluded.

In the new study researchers led by Andreas Schmittner from Oregon State University focused on the climate during the last ice age, about 19,000 to 23,000 years ago, to estimate how sensitive the climate system is to changing amounts of CO_2 (in the ice age scenario, a reduction of CO_2 helped cool the globe).

Boosting the amount of [greenhouse] gases in the atmosphere can warm the globe, whereas reducing them can plunge the planet into a deep freeze.

What they found was that climate models run with a high degree of climate sensitivity overestimated the cooling that occurred during the time period, depicting a planet completely encased in ice, when in fact evidence shows the tropics and sub-tropics were largely-ice free. Also, models with low climate sensitivity underestimated the cooling during that period.

"If these paleoclimatic constraints apply to the future, as predicted by our model, the results imply less probability of extreme climatic change than previously thought," Schmittner stated in a press release. He cautioned that climate change is nonetheless likely to have major consequences, even if it is not as extreme.

Greenhouse gases, such as CO_2, and nitrous oxide, are a key regulator of the planet's climate system. Boosting the amount of these gases in the atmosphere can warm the globe, whereas reducing them can plunge the planet into a deep freeze.

A useful way to think about CO_2 and other greenhouse gases comes from climate scientist Richard Alley of Penn State University, who is one of the foremost experts in paleoclimatology. He refers to carbon dioxide as the "biggest control knob" of the earth's climate.

Right now, human activities, such as burning coal for energy, are adding greenhouse gases to the atmosphere at such a rapid rate that we're well on our way to doubling the amount of CO_2 in the atmosphere compared to the preindustrial era—from 280 parts per million back then to about 389 parts per million now.

One of Many Studies

Before trumpeting the study's conclusions as an indication that climate change concerns are overblown, as some climate change skeptics have done, it's important to keep in mind that this is one of many studies that have examined the planet's likely response to a buildup in greenhouse gases. In fact, the question of exactly how warm the planet would get if the atmospheric concentration of CO_2 were to double is one that researchers have tackled for centuries.

In 1896, Swedish physical chemist Svante Arrhenius used longhand algebra to arrive at his conclusions regarding the sensitivity of the climate system. In his insightful book "The Discovery of Global Warming," science historian Spencer Weart describes Arrhenius's contributions:

> The prize sought by Arrhenius was the solution to the riddle of the ice ages. He focused on a decrease in CO_2 as a possible cause of cooling, and found that cutting the level in half could indeed bring an ice age. But he also took the trouble to estimate what might happen if the amount of gas in the atmosphere, at some distant time in the past or future, was double its present value. He computed that would bring roughly 5 or 6°C of global warming.

> This result is not far from the range that scientists would compute a century later using vastly better models—the current estimate is that a doubling of CO_2 will bring some 3 degrees of warming, give or take a degree or two. Did Arrhenius end up in the same range by sheer luck? Partly, but not entirely. In the sort of simple physics and chemistry calculations where Arrhenius had made his name, you can expect to come out roughly right if you address a powerful physical effect in a straightforward way, starting with decent data. . . .

Other noteworthy findings on climate sensitivity include the 1979 Charney Report from the National Academy of Sciences, which included a climate sensitivity estimate of 1.5 to 4.5°C. The most recent assessment from the U.N. Intergovernmental Panel on Climate Change (IPCC) contained the following language on climate sensitivity:

> Progress since the TAR [Third Assessment Report] enables an assessment that climate sensitivity is likely to be in the range of 2 to 4.5°C with a best estimate of about 3°C, and is very unlikely to be less than 1.5°C. Values substantially higher than 4.5°C cannot be excluded, but agreement of models with observations is not as good for those values.

The new study [of global warming models] also contains ... uncertainties, including the fact that the dataset the researchers used only included 26 percent of the planet's surface.

The IPCC mentioned several sources of uncertainty behind these estimates, including changes in cloud cover and type that could act to amplify or dampen global warming.

The new study also contains these and other uncertainties, including the fact that the dataset the researchers used only included 26 percent of the planet's surface. In addition, the new study found a surprisingly small temperature difference between average ocean temperatures during the last glacial maximum and today—just 2.6°C. This is not consistent with other studies, as the website Skeptical Science points out.

At the end of the day, this new study is another contribution to the long history of research on this topic, and may not even be much of a departure from the previous consensus view. Rather than a sharp break with the IPCC's 2007 findings, over at Eric Berger's "SciGuy" blog, Texas A&M University climate scientist Andrew Dessler says he views the new study as largely consistent with previous climate sensitivity estimates.

"Ordinarily, when something is published in *Science*, you expect it to be a significant advance/revision of our prior knowledge. I'm not sure that's the case here," Dessler stated. "My sense is that most scientists consider the very high end of the sensitivity range (greater than 4°C) to be pretty unlikely (although it cannot be ruled out), and the most likely value for climate sensitivity is around, probably slightly below, 3°C."

The BEST Study Did Not Address Whether Humans Are Causing Global Warming

Peter Ferrara

Peter Ferrara is a senior policy adviser at the Institute for Policy Innovation, a conservative think tank, and general counsel for the American Civil Rights Union, a conservative civil rights organization.

If you read this column completely and carefully today, you will learn about the true state of the scientific debate over global warming. You will not get the truth about that from the *Washington Post*, the *New York Times*, or the rest of the self-regarded "establishment" media. They are devoted to the fun and games of play acting as if there is no legitimate scientific debate over whether mankind's use of low cost, reliable energy from oil, coal and natural gas portends catastrophic global warming that threatens life on the planet as we know it.

Recently, the media Knights Templar of the religious orthodoxy of man-caused global warming made a contrived pass at reviving flagging public respect for their fading catechism. The occasion was massively overhyped and misrepresented reporting of the Berkeley Earth Surface Temperature (BEST) project. But all that was new from that project was the departures from the official catechism.

Nothing New in the BEST Study

The project reported only on the recorded temperature history since 1950 from temperature stations on land, which covers less than 30% of the earth's surface. As the project leader

Berkeley Professor Richard Muller reported in a *Wall Street Journal* commentary on October 21, [2011,] after obtaining and reviewing "more than 1.6 billion measurements from 39,000 [land based] temperature stations around the world ... the result showed [drum roll please] a temperature increase similar to that found by other groups." Those are most prominently NASA [National Aeronautics and Space Administration] and the National Oceanic and Atmospheric Administration in the U.S., and the Met Office and Climatic Research Unit in the United Kingdom.

In other words, that is nothing new. But this review and confirmation of the established land based temperature records that everyone working on the issue is familiar with was widely celebrated in the liberal/left Democrat Party controlled media as definitive new proof of the truth of the man-caused global warming religion.

Muller, however, was more intellectually honest than any of them in confessing in the *Journal* article that the BEST project involves no independent assessment of the question of "how much of the warming is due to humans and what will be the likely effects." But that is the whole issue in the global warming debate.

Muller's Concessions

Muller also honestly admits that "the [land based] temperature station quality is largely awful," noting that "a careful survey of these stations by a team led by meteorologist Anthony Watts showed that 70% of these stations have such poor siting that, by the U.S. government's own measure, they result in temperature uncertainties of between two and five degrees Celsius or more. We do not know how much worse are the stations in the developing world." He adds that, "The margin of error for the stations is at least three times larger than the estimated warming."

He also admits that the land based temperature records are corrupted by urban heat island distortions which are constantly growing over time, building in a warming bias. He recognizes that the established temperature authorities mentioned above today use data from only about 2,000 weather stations, down from 6,000 in 1970, which raises questions about their selections among available sites.

Scientifically recognized temperature proxy data from tree rings, ice cores, lake and ocean sediments, and stalagmites . . . show no warming since 1940.

Moreover, Muller admits the recognized temperature authorities try to homogenize the temperature records from the thousands of temperature stations around the globe to come up with a summary statistic of the degree of global warming, and serious questions can be raised as to how to do that, disputing a large portion of the warming attributed to humans. Muller also confesses that one-third of land based temperature stations worldwide show cooling rather than warming.

These concessions are important to recount because of more basic problems with the established land based temperature record that Muller doesn't confess. Weather satellites measuring atmospheric temperatures worldwide, over land and water, which are not subject to the above troubles of land based weather stations, show no warming since their record began in 1979, and before that there was actually global cooling dating back to 1940. The satellite record regarding atmospheric temperatures is independently confirmed by weather balloons. Moreover, the computer based climate models utilized by the UN's own Intergovernmental Panel on Climate Change (IPCC), and the atmospheric theory they rely upon, all insist that if man's use of carbon based fuels was warming the planet, the atmosphere must be warming faster than the surface.

In addition, the scientifically recognized temperature proxy data from tree rings, ice cores, lake and ocean sediments, and stalagmites also show no warming since 1940. Note that the warming before 1940 is attributable to the global recovery of temperatures from the Little Ice Age, and even the land based records show no warming over the last 13 years.

Fred Singer concludes as a result, "It is very likely that the reported warming during 1978–97 [from land based weather stations] is simply an artifact—the result of the measurement scheme rather than an actual warming." When Singer sent a letter to the editor to the global warming cheerleading *Washington Post*, pointing out the above anomalies and his conclusion, he reports the peculiar response that "they were willing to publish my letter, but not my credentials as emeritus professor at the University of Virginia and former director of the U.S. Weather Satellite Service. Apparently, they were concerned that readers might gain the impression that I knew something about climate."

Natural Causes for Warming

But there is more. Even the land based temperature record is not consistent with the theory of man-caused global warming. That record does not show persistent warming following persistent growth of CO_2 and other greenhouse gases. Rather, it shows an up and down pattern of temperatures more consistent with natural causes. Those include solar flare and sun spot cycles, and the periodic cycling of warm and cold water in the oceans from top to bottom, particularly the Pacific Decadal Oscillation (PDO).

The truth is a vigorous global scientific debate persists over whether man's use of carbon-based fuels threatens to cause catastrophic global warming, and the media not reporting that is not performing journalism. The most authoritative presentation of this debate can be found in the 856 page *Climate Change Reconsidered*, published by the Heartland Institute [a conservative think tank] in 2009. This careful, thoroughly scientific volume co-authored by dozens of fully credentialed scientists comprehensively addresses every aspect of global warming, and indicates that natural causes are primarily responsible for climate patterns of the last century. Heartland has just published a follow up 416 page Interim Report updating the debate.

Temperature changes predicted by the UN's global warming models over the past 20 years have been . . . much greater than the actual measured temperature changes.

When you run across a Knight Templar threatening you with a lance and a sword unless you confess the truth of catastrophic man-caused global warming, ask him for his rebuttal to *Climate Change Reconsidered.* You will find the effect is like showing a cross to a vampire.

Indeed, the latest and best work actually provides scientific proof that the man-caused global warming catechism is false. Fully documented work by Roy Spencer, U.S. Science Team Leader for the AMSR-E instrument flying on NASA's Aqua satellite, and Principal Research Scientist for the Earth Systems Science Center at the University of Alabama at Huntsville, shows using atmospheric temperature data from NASA's Terra satellite that much more heat escapes back out to space than is assumed captured in the atmosphere by greenhouse effects under the UN's theoretical climate models. This explains why the warming temperature changes predicted by the UN's global warming models over the past 20 years have been so much greater than the actual measured temperature changes.

In August, 2011 came the results of a major experiment by the European Organization for Nuclear Research (CERN), involving 63 scientists from 17 European and U.S. institutes. The results show that the sun's cosmic rays resulting from sunspots have a much greater effect on Earth's temperatures through their effect on cloud cover than the UN's global warming models have been assuming. This helps to explain why the historical pattern of temperature changes seems to follow the rise and fall of sunspots, rather than the concentration of CO_2 in the atmosphere. This further confirms what Heartland's *Climate Change Reconsidered* argues—that natural causes have the dominant effect on Earth's temperatures, not greenhouse gases.

Finally, the UN's own climate models project that if man's greenhouse gas emissions were causing global warming, there would be a particular pattern of temperature distribution in the atmosphere, which scientists call "the fingerprint." Temperatures in the troposphere portion of the atmosphere above the tropics would increase with altitude producing a "hotspot" near the top of the troposphere, about 6 miles above the earth's surface. Above that, in the stratosphere, there would be cooling. But higher quality temperature data from weather balloons and satellites now show just the opposite: no increasing warming with altitude in the tropical troposphere, but rather a slight cooling, with no hotspot, no fingerprint.

So the scientific foundation for shutting down our modern, 21st century, industrial economy has been obliterated. But that is not stopping religious crusaders, due to the extremist ideology and special interests driving the global warming charade.

The BEST Study
Hid the Critical Fact
That Global Warming Has
Stopped in Recent Years

David Rose

David Rose is a reporter for the Daily Mail, *a British tabloid.*

It was hailed as the scientific study that ended the global warming debate once and for all—the research that, in the words of its director, 'proved you should not be a sceptic, at least not any longer'.

Professor Richard Muller, of Berkeley University in California, and his colleagues from the Berkeley Earth Surface Temperatures project team (BEST) claimed to have shown that the planet has warmed by almost a degree centigrade since 1950 and is warming continually.

Published last week [October 21, 2011,] ahead of a major United Nations climate summit in Durban, South Africa, next month, their work was cited around the world as irrefutable evidence that only the most stringent measures to reduce carbon dioxide emissions can save civilisation as we know it.

It was cited uncritically by, among others, reporters and commentators from the BBC, *The Independent*, *The Guardian*, *The Economist* and numerous media outlets in America.

The *Washington Post* said the BEST study had 'settled the climate change debate' and showed that anyone who remained a sceptic was committing a 'cynical fraud'.

But today [October 30, 2011,] *The Mail on Sunday* can reveal that a leading member of Prof Muller's team has accused him of trying to mislead the public by hiding the fact that BEST's research shows global warming has stopped.

Prof Judith Curry, who chairs the Department of Earth and Atmospheric Sciences at America's prestigious Georgia Institute of Technology, said that Prof Muller's claim that he has proven global warming sceptics wrong was also a 'huge mistake', with no scientific basis.

[BEST researcher Judith] Curry said the project's research data show there has been no increase in world temperatures since the end of the Nineties.

Prof Curry is a distinguished climate researcher with more than 30 years experience and the second named co-author of the BEST project's four research papers.

Her comments, in an exclusive interview with *The Mail on Sunday*, seem certain to ignite a furious academic row. She said this affair had to be compared to the notorious 'Climategate' scandal [in 2009].

Like the scientists exposed then by leaked emails from East Anglia University's Climatic Research Unit, her colleagues from the BEST project seem to be trying to 'hide the decline' in rates of global warming.

In fact, Prof Curry said, the project's research data show there has been no increase in world temperatures since the end of the Nineties—a fact confirmed by a new analysis that *The Mail on Sunday* has obtained.

'There is no scientific basis for saying that warming hasn't stopped,' she said. 'To say that there is detracts from the credibility of the data, which is very unfortunate.'

However, Prof Muller denied warming was at a standstill.

'We see no evidence of it [global warming] having slowed down,' he told *BBC Radio 4's Today* programme. There was, he added, 'no levelling off'.

A graph issued by the BEST project also suggests a continuing steep increase.

But a report to be published today by the Global Warming Policy Foundation includes a graph of world average temperatures over the past ten years, drawn from the BEST project's data and revealed on its website.

This graph shows that the trend of the last decade is absolutely flat, with no increase at all—though the levels of carbon dioxide in the atmosphere have carried on rising relentlessly.

'This is nowhere near what the climate models were predicting,' Prof Curry said. 'Whatever it is that's going on here, it doesn't look like it's being dominated by CO_2.'

No Reason to End Scepticism

Prof Muller also wrote an article for the *Wall Street Journal*. It was here, under the headline 'The case against global warming scepticism', that he proclaimed 'there were good reasons for doubt until now'.

This, too, went around the world, with *The Economist*, among many others, stating there was now 'little room for doubt'.

Such claims left Prof Curry horrified.

'Of course this isn't the end of scepticism,' she said. 'To say that is the biggest mistake he [Prof Muller] has made. When I saw he was saying that I just thought, "Oh my God".'

In fact, she added, in the wake of the unexpected global warming standstill, many climate scientists who had previously rejected sceptics' arguments were now taking them much more seriously.

They were finally addressing questions such as the influence of clouds, natural temperature cycles and solar radiation—as they should have done, she said, a long time ago.

Yesterday Prof Muller insisted that neither his claims that there has not been a standstill, nor the graph, were misleading because the project had made its raw data available on its website, enabling others to draw their own graphs.

However, he admitted it was true that the BEST data suggested that world temperatures have not risen for about 13 years. But in his view, this might not be 'statistically significant', although, he added, it was equally possible that it was—a statement which left other scientists mystified.

'I am baffled as to what he's trying to do,' Prof Curry said.

Prof Ross McKittrick, a climate statistics expert from Guelph University in Ontario, added: 'You don't look for statistically significant evidence of a standstill.

'You look for statistically significant evidence of change.'

The BEST project, which has been lavishly funded, brings together experts from different fields from top American universities.

It was set up 18 months ago [in spring of 2010] in an effort to devise a new and more accurate way of computing changes in world temperatures by using readings from some 39,000 weather stations on land, instead of adding sea temperatures as well.

You don't look for statistically significant evidence of a standstill. You look for statistically significant evidence of change.

Some scientists, Prof Muller included, believe that this should provide a more accurate indication of how the world is responding to carbon dioxide.

The oceans, they argue, warm more slowly and this is why earlier global measurements which also cover the sea—such as those from the Climatic Research Unit at East Anglia University—have found no evidence of warming since the Nineties.

The usual way a high-profile project such as BEST would publish its results would be in a scientific journal, following a rigorous 'peer review' by other experts in the field.

The more eminent journals that publish climate research, such as *Nature* and *Science*, insist there must be no leaks to the media until this review is complete and if such leaks occur, they will automatically reject the research.

Earlier this year [2011], the project completed four research papers.

As well as trends in world temperatures, they looked at the extent to which temperature readings can be distorted by urban 'heat islands' and the influence of long-term temperature cycles in the oceans. The papers were submitted to the *Journal of Geophysical Research*.

Sabotaging Peer Review Process

But although Prof Curry is the second named author of all four papers, Prof Muller failed to consult her before deciding to put them on the internet earlier this month, when the peer review process had barely started, and to issue a detailed press release at the same time.

He also briefed selected journalists individually. 'It is not how I would have played it,' Prof Curry said. 'I was informed only when I got a group email. I think they have made errors and I distance myself from what they did.

'It would have been smart to consult me.' She said it was unfortunate that although the *Journal of Geophysical Research* had allowed Prof Muller to issue the papers, the reviewers were, under the journal's policy, forbidden from public comment.

Prof McKittrick added: 'The fact is that many of the people who are in a position to provide informed criticism of this work are currently bound by confidentiality agreements.

'For the Berkeley team to have chosen this particular moment to launch a major international publicity blitz is a highly unethical sabotage of the peer review process.'

In Prof Curry's view, two of the papers were not ready to be published, in part because they did not properly address the arguments of climate sceptics.

As for the graph disseminated to the media, she said: 'This is "hide the decline" stuff. Our data show the pause, just as the other sets of data do. Muller is hiding the decline.

'To say this is the end of scepticism is misleading, as is the statement that warming hasn't paused. It is also misleading to say, as he has, that the issue of heat islands has been settled.'

Prof Muller said she was 'out of the loop'. He added: 'I wasn't even sent the press release before it was issued.'

Prof Muller defended his behaviour yesterday, saying that all he was doing was 'returning to traditional peer review', issuing draft papers to give the whole 'climate community' a chance to comment.

As for the press release, he claimed he was 'not seeking publicity', adding: 'This is simply a way of getting the media to report this more accurately.'

He said his decision to publish was completely unrelated to the forthcoming United Nations climate conference.

This, he said, was 'irrelevant', insisting that nothing could have been further from his mind than trying to influence it.

The CERN Study Demonstrates That Nature, Not Humans, Controls the Earth's Temperatures

Chriss W. Street

Chriss W. Street is a financial writer and a blogger at Biggovern-ment.com, a conservative political website.

*N*ature Journal of Science, ranked as the world's most cited scientific periodical, has just published the definitive study on Global Warming that proves the dominant controller of temperatures in the Earth's atmosphere is due to galactic cosmic rays and the sun, rather than by man. One of the report's authors, Professor Jyrki Kauppinen, summed up his conclusions regarding the potential for man-made Global Warming: "I think it is such a blatant falsification."

The research was conducted by CERN, the European Organization for Nuclear Research, which invented the World Wide Web, built the multi-billion dollar Large Hadron Collider, and now has constructed a pristinely clean stainless steel chamber that precisely recreates the Earth's atmosphere. The climate study involved scientists representing 17 of Europe's and America's premiere research institutes. The results demonstrate that cosmic rays promote the formation of molecules that can grow and seed clouds in the Earth's atmosphere; the temperatures then fall as the density of the clouds increase. Because the sun's magnetic field controls how many cosmic rays reach Earth's atmosphere; the sun determines the temperature on Earth.

Nature Journal has been the holy-grail of scientific research publication since it was established in England in 1869. Its original editors gave the title to their new scientific journal in celebration of a line by British poet William Wordsworth: "To the solid ground of nature trusts the Mind that builds for aye". Because research scientists are the primary audience [for] this most prestigious of journals, the magazine strives to retain its stamp of approval as the pinnacle of scientific credibility for original research. *Nature* first introduced its readers to X-rays, DNA double helix, wave nature of particles, pulsars, and more recently mapping of the human genome.

But *Nature*'s reputation suffered a huge black eye on November 21, 2009 when a hacker broke into the computers at the University of East Anglia's Climate Research Unit (CRU) and released 1079 e-mails and 72 documents exposing willful fraud in several scientific papers published in *Nature* that supported [former US vice president] Al Gore's theory of Anthropogenic Global Warming. CRU houses the world's most extensive data base on atmospheric temperatures and the e-mails exposed blatant exaggerations of the warming data, possible illegal destruction of evidence, and conspiracy to manipulate or suppress data not supporting of the man-made Global Warming theory.

E-mail Evidence

One e-mail describes tricks used supporting Anthropogenics in a major *Nature* article:

> "I've just completed Mike's *Nature* trick of adding in the real temps to each series for the last 20 years (ie from 1981 onwards) and from 1961 for Keith's to hide the decline."

As the *Wall Street Journal* and other conservative media hyper-ventilated over the hacker leaks they referred to as the "Climategate Scandal", *Nature* quickly retaliated in defense of Anthropogenic Global Warming with a scathing editorial titled: "Climatologists Under Pressure" stating: "Stolen e-mails have revealed no scientific conspiracy, but do highlight ways in which climate researchers could be better supported in the face of public scrutiny." The editorial skewered academic doubters of man-made Global Warming as the "climate-change-denialist fringe" and in a shocking Freudian-slip the *Nature* editorial roared its political partisanship:

> "This paranoid interpretation would be laughable were it not for the fact that obstructionist politicians in the US Senate will probably use it next year as an excuse to stiffen their opposition to the country's much needed climate bill. Nothing in the e-mails undermines the scientific case that global warming is real—or that human activities are almost certainly the cause."

After 20 years of academic supremacy and hundreds of billions of dollars of costs; the Anthropogenic Global Warming theory seems headed for the dust bin of history.

For *Nature* to now publish research that eviscerates the Anthropogenics theory heralds a tectonic rejection by academia of support for United Nations Framework Convention on Climate Change. The UN protocol requires every nation on earth to reduce their atmospheric emissions of greenhouse gas to 94.8% of 1990 levels to "prevent dangerous anthropogenic interference with the climate system." The U.S. Senate legislation that *Nature* [is] . . . stridently lobbying for is named "America's Climate Security Act of 2007", commonly known as the Cap-and-Trade Bill.

The Heritage Foundation estimated that the costs of complying with Cap-and-Trade would include; a 29% increase in the price of gasoline, losses of hundreds of thousands of jobs, and lead to reductions of $1.7 to $4.8 trillion of the U.S. GDP [gross domestic product] by 2030. Furthermore, Cap-and-Trade would set up a gargantuan intergovernmental bureaucracy that would likely ban natural gas tracking, steam injection of tar sands, and surface coal mining for exploration and development of America's immense energy reserves.

After 20 years of academic supremacy and hundreds of billions of dollars of costs; the Anthropogenic Global Warming theory seems headed for the dust bin of history. Perhaps the admirable action of the *Nature Journal of Science* to place scientific integrity above partisan politics will be a valuable lesson for the scientific community in the future.

The Science Shows There Will Be No Apocalyptic Global Warming

Patrick Michaels

Patrick Michaels is a senior fellow in climate studies at the Cato Institute, a libertarian think tank. He also contributed as an author and reviewer of the United Nations Intergovernmental Panel on Climate Change, an international scientific body charged with investigating climate change.

We now have a full one-third of a century of satellite-measured lower atmospheric temperatures, and what an interesting story the machines are revealing! I think it's fair to say that they provide increasing evidence in favor of the "lukewarm" view of climate change, or the hypothesis of modest warming. In climate change, "it's not the heat, it's the sensitivity," or the amount of warming that a change in carbon dioxide causes, that is important.

Almost every map of the decadal trends in the satellite data is centered on the Equator. . . . But much more interesting things are going on around the poles, where the climate action is.

For a number of reasons, computer models with added atmospheric carbon dioxide preferentially warm the mid-and high-latitude land areas of the northern hemisphere that are ice-free, which also enhances summer melting of the relatively shallow ice in the Arctic Ocean. That, in turn, results in an increased absorption of solar radiation by the darker ocean surface, which also contributes to warming. . . .

The warming of high-latitude North America and the adjacent Arctic Ocean is the largest of any on the planet. Note that there tends to be less warming over the massive Greenland ice cap.

That's because Greenland is kind of a miniature Antarctica, where things are much different than they are in our hemisphere. . . .

The models aren't even close in the amount of warming.

Antarctica is surrounded by a very cold and turbulent ocean, whose massive thermal capacity (compared to land) drastically reduces warming, compared to what we see in our hemisphere. But, even a tiny warming of the huge Southern Ocean must increase the amount of moisture in the air around Antarctica which can only result in more clouds and snow over the continent. Indeed, interior Antarctica can conceivably cool with a modest "global" warming. Warming doomsayers conveniently ignore the fact that even the UN's models (current version) forecast that Antarctica will gain ice this century.

A lot of interior Antarctica (and a big patch of the Southern Ocean, for reasons I think no one understands) is getting colder. There are some pockets of decent maritime warming right near the coast, which almost certainly are increasing snowfall substantially when the wind blows onshore.

Here's the lukewarm part: The bipolar behavior is pretty close—in pattern—to what theory and models say should be happening. But the models aren't even close in the amount of warming.

The average warming trend in the one-third century of satellite data is 0.14°C per decade, but the warming rate in the UN's midrange climate models is 0.25°. This differential has been pretty constant ever since the satellite data was corrected for orbital and sensor issues.

There's no reason for that not to continue. In other words, the UN's average forecast of 3.2°C of warming this century is off by about 40%, which should spell the victory of the luke-warmers and the death-knell of apocalyptic global warming. Indeed, it is not the heat, it's the sensitivity, which looks to be quite a bit lower than what's in those computer simulations.

CHAPTER 2

Are Global Warming Skeptics Motivated by Science?

Chapter Preface

Some of the most damaging attacks on global warming science occurred following a hacking of computers at the Climatic Research Unit (CRU) at the University of East Anglia in the United Kingdom, and the release in November 2009 of thousands of e-mails exchanged between climate researchers. Some of the e-mails appeared to suggest that certain prominent climate scientists may have manipulated climate data to make average global temperature increases look worse than the data supported. Global warming skeptics trumpeted the news, claiming that it undermined global warming science, and the ensuing scandal became known as Climategate.

The focus of the e-mails was the presentation of historical temperature data collected by three highly respected scientific bodies—the CRU (in conjunction with the Hadley Centre for Climate Prediction and Research), the NASA Goddard Institute for Space Studies (GISS) series, and the National Oceanic and Atmospheric Administration (NOAA). Climate change skeptics pointed to e-mails sent by Tom Wigley of the National Center for Atmospheric Research and the head of CRU, Phil Jones. In one e-mail, Wigley suggested lowering mid-twentieth century temperatures by .15 degrees Celsius in order to make the later temperature increases look bigger. Jones responded in another e-mail, characterizing Wigley's proposal as a trick to hide tree ring data suggesting that temperatures had actually declined instead of increased. A graphic employing the adjusted data and showing a recent sharp increase in Northern Hemisphere temperatures was published as part of a publication by the World Meteorological Association in 1999. Global warming skeptics argued that this amounted to a misrepresentation of scientific data, suggesting that scientists were willing to subvert science to win the public relations battle over climate change. This, skeptics said, called into question the entire global warming theory. Climate scientists, on the other hand, objected that the e-mails were taken entirely out of context and argued that nothing in the messages affected the fundamental science on global warming.

The hacker who started the Climategate scandal was never identified, but numerous governmental and scholarly investigations were conducted to determine whether there was fraud, scientific misconduct, or any reason to doubt climate science as a result of the scandal. Investigations, for example, were conducted by the British government, the University of Pennsylvania, independent scientific organizations and commissions, and the US Environmental Protection Agency (EPA). None of the investigations found any evidence of fraud or scientific misconduct, and although some reports criticized climate scientists for a lack of transparency, nothing was found to cast doubt on the scientific consensus that global warming is occurring and is the result of human activity. A statement issued by the EPA on July 29, 2010, is representative. In it, the EPA explained that the agency was denying petitions challenging its previous climate change findings because "climate science is credible, compelling, and growing stronger," and because "EPA reviewed every [Climategate] e-mail and found this was simply a candid discussion of scientists working through issues that arise in compiling and presenting large complex data sets."[1]

A recent study, many commentators claim, may have bolstered the findings of the Climategate investigations. University of California at Berkeley physicist Richard Muller—himself a skeptic about whether the Climategate e-mails uncovered a possible inaccuracy in temperature data used to support global-warming theory—decided to conduct independent research to test the quality of temperature data. Among Muller's concerns, for example, was that weather stations may be reporting unusually high temperatures due to their location in hot urban areas. Muller established the Berkeley Earth Surface

Temperature (BEST) Project to conduct the research, looking at raw temperature data from more than thirty-nine thousand measuring sites—many more than were used in previous climate research. On October 20, 2011, BEST issued a press release basically concluding that global warming is real and that the research done by climate scientists was accurate.

The most recent scandal in the public relations war about global warming involved a leak of anti-global-warming documents from the Heartland Institute, a free-market think tank known for its criticisms of global-warming science. Some of the documents revealed that the BEST Project was receiving funds from the Charles G. Koch Foundation, an oil-industry-funded group that denies global warming and opposes clean energy and climate legislation. Another document, which Heartland claims is fake, detailed a strategy to push classroom curriculums that teach that climate science is controversial and uncertain. Some commentators said the Heartland scandal revealed that global-warming skeptics simply want to undermine legitimate climate science, while others noted that Heartland is an advocacy group and that the released documents showed no type of legal misconduct. The authors of the viewpoints in this chapter debate the motivations of global-warming skeptics.

Notes

1. Environmental Protection Agency, "EPA Rejects Claims of Flawed Climate Science," July 29, 2010. http://yosemite .epa.gov/opa/admpress.nsf/0/56EB0D86757CB7568525776 F0063D82F.

The Number of Scientists Questioning Global Warming Is Growing

Claude Allegre et al.

Claude Allegre is the former director of the Institute for the Study of the Earth at the University of Paris. The following opinion piece, originally published in the Wall Street Journal, *was written and signed by Allegre and fifteen other scientists, all of whom are listed at the end of the viewpoint.*

A candidate for public office in any contemporary democracy may have to consider what, if anything, to do about "global warming." Candidates should understand that the oft-repeated claim that nearly all scientists demand that something dramatic be done to stop global warming is not true. In fact, a large and growing number of distinguished scientists and engineers do not agree that drastic actions on global warming are needed.

In September [2011], Nobel Prize–winning physicist Ivar Giaever, a supporter of President [Barack] Obama in the last election, publicly resigned from the American Physical Society (APS) with a letter that begins: "I did not renew [my membership] because I cannot live with the [APS policy] statement: 'The evidence is incontrovertible: Global warming is occurring. If no mitigating actions are taken, significant disruptions in the Earth's physical and ecological systems, social systems, security and human health are likely to occur. We must reduce emissions of greenhouse gases beginning now.' In the APS it is OK to discuss whether the mass of the proton changes over time and how a multi-universe behaves, but the evidence of global warming is incontrovertible?"

In spite of a multidecade international campaign to enforce the message that increasing amounts of the "pollutant" carbon dioxide will destroy civilization, large numbers of scientists, many very prominent, share the opinions of Dr. Giaever. And the number of scientific "heretics" is growing with each passing year. The reason is a collection of stubborn scientific facts.

The lack of warming for more than a decade . . . suggests that computer models have greatly exaggerated how much warming additional CO_2 can cause.

Perhaps the most inconvenient fact is the lack of global warming for well over 10 years now. This is known to the warming establishment, as one can see from the 2009 "Climategate" email of climate scientist Kevin Trenberth: "The fact is that we can't account for the lack of warming at the moment and it is a travesty that we can't." But the warming is only missing if one believes computer models where so-called feedbacks involving water vapor and clouds greatly amplify the small effect of CO_2 [carbon dioxide].

The lack of warming for more than a decade—indeed, the smaller-than-predicted warming over the 22 years since the U.N.'s Intergovernmental Panel on Climate Change (IPCC) began issuing projections—suggests that computer models have greatly exaggerated how much warming additional CO_2 can cause. Faced with this embarrassment, those promoting alarm have shifted their drumbeat from warming to weather extremes, to enable anything unusual that happens in our chaotic climate to be ascribed to CO_2.

The fact is that CO_2 is not a pollutant. CO_2 is a colorless and odorless gas, exhaled at high concentrations by each of us, and a key component of the biosphere's life cycle. Plants do so much better with more CO_2 that greenhouse operators often increase the CO_2 concentrations by factors of three or four to get better growth. This is no surprise since plants and animals evolved when CO_2 concentrations were about 10 times larger than they are today. Better plant varieties, chemical fertilizers and agricultural management contributed to the great increase in agricultural yields of the past century, but part of the increase almost certainly came from additional CO_2 in the atmosphere.

Pressure on Scientists

Although the number of publicly dissenting scientists is growing, many young scientists furtively say that while they also have serious doubts about the global-warming message, they are afraid to speak up for fear of not being promoted—or worse. They have good reason to worry. In 2003, Dr. Chris de Freitas, the editor of the journal *Climate Research*, dared to publish a peer-reviewed article with the politically incorrect (but factually correct) conclusion that the recent warming is not unusual in the context of climate changes over the past thousand years. The international warming establishment quickly mounted a determined campaign to have Dr. de Freitas removed from his editorial job and fired from his university position. Fortunately, Dr. de Freitas was able to keep his university job.

This is not the way science is supposed to work, but we have seen it before—for example, in the frightening period when Trofim Lysenko hijacked biology in the Soviet Union. Soviet biologists who revealed that they believed in genes, which Lysenko maintained were a bourgeois fiction, were fired from their jobs. Many were sent to the gulag [prison camps] and some were condemned to death.

Why is there so much passion about global warming, and why has the issue become so vexing that the American Physical Society, from which Dr. Giaever resigned a few months ago, refused the seemingly reasonable request by many of its members to remove the word "incontrovertible" from its description of a scientific issue? There are several reasons, but a good place to start is the old question "cui bono?" ["who benefits?"] Or the modern update, "Follow the money."

The highest benefit-to-cost ratio is achieved for a [climate-change] policy that allows 50 more years of economic growth unimpeded by greenhouse gas controls.

Alarmism over climate is of great benefit to many, providing government funding for academic research and a reason for government bureaucracies to grow. Alarmism also offers an excuse for governments to raise taxes, taxpayer-funded subsidies for businesses that understand how to work the political system, and a lure for big donations to charitable foundations promising to save the planet. Lysenko and his team lived very well, and they fiercely defended their dogma and the privileges it brought them.

Speaking for many scientists and engineers who have looked carefully and independently at the science of climate, we have a message to any candidate for public office: There is no compelling scientific argument for drastic action to "decarbonize" the world's economy. Even if one accepts the inflated climate forecasts of the IPCC, aggressive greenhouse-gas control policies are not justified economically.

A recent study of a wide variety of policy options by Yale economist William Nordhaus showed that nearly the highest benefit-to-cost ratio is achieved for a policy that allows 50 more years of economic growth unimpeded by greenhouse gas controls. This would be especially beneficial to the less-developed parts of the world that would like to share some of the same advantages of material well-being, health and life expectancy that the fully developed parts of the world enjoy now. Many other policy responses would have a negative return on investment. And it is likely that more CO_2 and the modest warming that may come with it will be an overall benefit to the planet.

A Need for Critical Review

If elected officials feel compelled to "do something" about climate, we recommend supporting the excellent scientists who are increasing our understanding of climate with well-designed instruments on satellites, in the oceans and on land, and in the analysis of observational data. The better we understand climate, the better we can cope with its ever-changing nature, which has complicated human life throughout history. However, much of the huge private and government investment in climate is badly in need of critical review.

Every candidate should support rational measures to protect and improve our environment, but it makes no sense at all to back expensive programs that divert resources from real needs and are based on alarming but untenable claims of "incontrovertible" evidence.

[Signed:] *Claude Allegre, former director of the Institute for the Study of the Earth, University of Paris; J. Scott Armstrong, cofounder of the Journal of Forecasting and the International Journal of Forecasting; Jan Breslow, head of the Laboratory of Biochemical Genetics and Metabolism, Rockefeller University; Roger Cohen, fellow, American Physical Society; Edward David, member, National Academy of Engineering and National Academy of Sciences; William Happer, professor of physics, Princeton; Michael Kelly, professor of technology, University of Cambridge, U.K.; William Kininmonth, former head of climate research at the Australian Bureau of Meteorology; Richard Lindzen, professor of atmospheric sciences, MIT; James McGrath, professor of chemistry, Virginia Technical University; Rodney Nichols, former president and CEO of the New York Academy of Sciences; Burt Rutan, aerospace engineer, designer of Voyager and Space-ShipOne; Harrison H. Schmitt, Apollo 17 astronaut and former*

U.S. senator; Nir Shaviv, professor of astrophysics, Hebrew University, Jerusalem; Henk Tennekes, former director, Royal Dutch Meteorological Service; Antonio Zichichi, president of the World Federation of Scientists, Geneva.

Global-Warming Science Is Merely a Working Hypothesis

Gary M. Vasey

Gary M. Vasey is an energy industry expert from the Czech Republic and managing director of European operations for Commodity Point, a research and analysis firm that focuses on issues affecting the wholesale trading of commodities.

If there is a single issue today that is bound to cause controversy and a reaction from our readers it has to be that of global warming. My past efforts at discussing this issue have always resulted in a lot of feedback from all sides of the debate. However, I want to tackle this topic again today, as it impacts our industry significantly.

The number of times I have seen the phrase "the science is proven" when it relates to the potential impact of manmade CO_2 [carbon dioxide] on the Earth's climate astonishes me. For some, the very fact that I even termed this a "debate" above will be enough—however, do please keep reading. But let us look at whether, in fact, the science is proven and we may find that idea that the "science is proven" or, even that the majority of scientists agree, is simply not true.

Science, as I was taught by the professor of Geological Sciences at the University of Strathclyde as I started my Ph.D., is about creating a working hypothesis that explains all of the observable facts. This working hypothesis must be presented for peer review by the community of scientists who will attempt to find flaws in it. If no flaws are immediately found, the hypothesis may be accepted as the best hypothesis available until such time as it fails to explain a new observation. At which time, it may be amended or scrapped in favor of a new hypothesis. In this way, science and scientists are progressively working towards the ultimate hypothesis but they may never actually know if they got there. There is no such thing as a proven hypothesis. There are just accepted (temporarily) hypotheses. We all know examples of this from our schooldays such as Newton's laws and how those were eventually modified and replaced by Einstein and others' improved theorems. We may even have read recently how scientists may have discovered particles that appear to break Einstein's laws.

The only factual thing we can prove relative to climate is what we already know to occur—that the Earth's climate changes.

In other words, a hypothesis is never actually "proven" and by suggesting that [it is] demonstrates a misunderstanding of what science actually is and how it is properly performed.

The problem with the global warming debate is that I (or anyone) can rightly say that they observe the effects of climate change on the world. "I see it with my own eyes." This statement is true—we do observe climate change all around us— but how this then must mean that man made CO_2 is responsible is, I would argue, based on a leap of faith. The Earth's climate isn't static, it changes through time both globally and regionally. Such changes may be observed in our lifetime as well as [in] the geological record. From a scientific perspective, over the course of our short lives about the only factual thing we can prove relative to climate is what we already know to occur—that the Earth's climate changes.

Logical reasoning suggests that, if the Earth's climate has always changed through time (more than four billion years of it), then we must look for the mechanisms behind those changes through that entire period of time. In other words, if nothing new is occurring now, then the answer to what drives climate change must be some broad set of systemic Earth processes. We even have some ideas about what these processes are. They include things like continental configuration, ocean currents, cloud formation and cover, solar activity, and much more. It's a very complex set of processes that are not entirely understood (i.e., the science of climate is, in fact, a long way from being "proven").

Why, then, the focus on CO_2? A gas that occupies such a minimal proportion (parts per million) of the planet's atmosphere that logical thought would immediately discount the idea that minor fluctuations of the stuff could cause much of an issue on a global scale. We also know that in the distant past the Earth's atmosphere contained significantly more CO_2 without much of a discernible impact on temperature. In fact, today, our atmosphere is actually CO_2-impoverished by comparison to the geologic past.

While [the CERN CLOUD finding] may not disprove the idea that CO_2 is responsible [for global warming], it casts further doubt on that theory.

For me, it intuitively feels wrong that CO_2, a gas for which Mother Earth appears to have many processes to regulate it (so-called carbon sinks) could possibly be the sole culprit? And while some may react strongly to my having this doubt, please keep in mind it is doubt that helps to drive better science. We must never stop asking ourselves, "Do we have this right? What can we do to continue to gather objective data and analysis?" This is the basis of good science.

Politics and Belief

The potential problem, as I see it, is that the question of climate change has become politicized to the point where criticisms or even critiques of analysis or data are met with an immediate dismissal or fierce opposition. Climate science has become anything but science with believers on both sides of the debate who seek to block the publication via peer review of opposing views, attempt to discredit each other both professionally and personally, and resort to the utilization of fear-making sound bites delivered via the global media. Research funding isn't readily available to those who seek to probe the currently accepted hypotheses.

A good example of this is the recent findings by The European Organization for Nuclear Research (CERN) published in *Nature* magazine. CERN has called for climate models to be changed in the light of its findings calling the findings rightly "politically sensitive." Why? because the research shows rather definitively that cosmic rays do seed clouds in the atmosphere which impacts climate change and this requires computer climate models to be overhauled. In the press briefing from CERN regarding the experiment, they said,

> Based on the first results from CLOUD [a study titled Cosmics Leaving Outdoor Droplets], it is clear that the treatment of aerosol formation in climate models will need to be substantially revised, since all models assume that nucleation is caused by these vapours and water alone. It is now urgent to identify the additional nucleating vapours, and whether their sources are mainly natural or from human activities.

CERN built a stainless steel chamber to as accurately as possible recreate the Earth's atmosphere to test the idea that clouds may be the *primary driver* of global climate as opposed to CO_2. It, therefore, tested the relative importance of one aspect of the factors involved in climate change outlined above. In this chamber, 63 CERN scientists from 17 European and American institutes demonstrated that cosmic rays promote the formation of molecules which grow in Earth's atmosphere and seed clouds, making it cloudier and cooler. While it may not disprove the idea that CO_2 is responsible, it casts further doubt on that theory.

But the real story here is just how politically complex it was for CERN to fund and conduct this experiment. In an intriguing article written by Lawrence Solomon for the *Financial Post*, we learn the truth behind this experiment. I quote verbatim.

> The hypothesis that cosmic rays and the sun hold the key to the global warming debate has been Enemy No. 1 to the global warming establishment ever since it was first proposed by two scientists from the Danish Space Research Institute, at a 1996 scientific conference in the U.K. [United Kingdom]. Within one day, the chairman of the Intergovernmental Panel on Climate Change [IPCC], Bert Bolin, denounced the theory, saying, "I find the move from this pair scientifically extremely naive and irresponsible." He then set about discrediting the theory, any journalist that gave the theory credence, and most of all the Danes presenting the theory—they soon found themselves vilified, marginalized and starved of funding, despite their impeccable scientific credentials.

> The mobilization to rally the press against the Danes worked brilliantly, with one notable exception. Nigel Calder, a former editor of *The New Scientist* who attended that 1996 conference, would not be cowed. Himself a physicist, Mr. Calder became convinced of the merits of the argument and a year later, following a lecture he gave at a CERN conference, so too did Jasper Kirkby, a CERN scientist in attendance. Mr. Kirkby then convinced the CERN bureaucracy of the theory's importance and developed a plan to create a cloud chamber—he called it CLOUD, for "Cosmics Leaving Outdoor Droplets."

> But Mr. Kirkby made the same tactical error that the Danes had—not realizing how politicized the global warming issue was, he candidly shared his views with the scientific community.

> "The theory will probably be able to account for somewhere between a half and the whole of the increase in the Earth's

temperature that we have seen in the last century," Mr. Kirkby told the scientific press in 1998, explaining that global warming may be part of a natural cycle in the Earth's temperature.

The global warming establishment sprang into action, pressured the Western governments that control CERN, and almost immediately succeeded in suspending CLOUD. It took Mr. Kirkby almost a decade of negotiation with his superiors, and who knows how many compromises and unspoken commitments, to convince the CERN bureaucracy to allow the project to proceed. And years more to create the cloud chamber and convincingly validate the Danes' groundbreaking theory.

Yet this spectacular success will be largely unrecognized by the general public for years—this column will be the first that most readers have heard of it—because CERN remains too afraid of offending its government masters to admit its success. Weeks ago, CERN formally decided to muzzle Mr. Kirby and other members of his team to avoid "the highly political arena of the climate change debate," telling them "to present the results clearly but not interpret them" and to downplay the results by "mak[ing] clear that cosmic radiation is only one of many parameters." The CERN study and press release is written in bureaucratese and the version of Mr. Kirkby's study that appears in the print edition of *Nature* censored the most eye-popping graph—only those who know where to look in an online supplement will see the striking potency of cosmic rays in creating the conditions for seeding clouds.

Continue to Test the Hypothesis

The implication that man made CO_2 is causing temperature increases and that it will result in calamitous impacts for mankind has many far-reaching consequences. Regulation of CO_2 emissions impacts each and every one of us and specifically our industry, including potentially higher taxes or costs and ultimately changes in lifestyle. Given that, we should be careful to be sure that these fundamental shifts in lifestyle and business processes are founded on proper science and debate. Other well-supported explanations for the observed changes in climate are emerging and they should not be rejected out of hand, but met with careful critique. The scientific method requires it.

Global-Warming Science Is New and Untested

Evan Sayet

Evan Sayet is a conservative satirist, political commentator, and political writer.

Let's begin by acknowledging that the science of global warming is beyond the vast majority of us. Nonetheless, this does not mean we turn off our brains and simply accept the pronouncements of those sounding the alarm and offering their remedies. I am a global warming skeptic (to say the least) specifically because I have thought through the issue and the claims of the alarmists just don't add up. What follows is my thinking and what it is that has led me to conclude that global-warming is a leftist farce which is being perpetuated for both financial and political reasons.

First, I am skeptical because skepticism is the scientific starting point. Not cynicism but skepticism. This is especially true when the remedy being proposed is so drastic—in this case requiring the near-total dismantling of society as we know it.

I am not overly impressed by talk of a "consensus" as there are enough good and serious scientists who reject the claims of the alarmists to make the pronouncement of "consensus" simply untrue. Besides, every wrong theory that had previously been embraced by society—such as the "fact" that the world is flat—was embraced by a "consensus" of scientists at the time and obviously that consensus was very wrong.

My skepticism is only increased with the knowledge that the science of climatology is relatively new, little tested and

since its claims about consequences are decades and even centuries in the future, never proven by having had their predictions come true. In fact, many of the alarmists' most hyped claims have been proved by time to be patently wrong. As one leading alarmist wrote in an email he thought would remain private, global warming has been on a fifteen year hiatus that he felt needed to be covered-up.

> *For as long as I can remember the "experts"—many the very same people pushing global warming hysteria today—have been predicting one ecological disaster after another.*

My skepticism of this new science is furthered even more by the knowledge that the "facts" upon which their models are created are based almost entirely on numbers that are not easily verified and which require great speculation to determine. If these "facts" are wrong then the models are useless (to say the least.) Remember, the whole global-warming theory is based on only a couple of degrees of change over many millennia. Do scientists *really* know what the temperature was in northeast Siberia in the year 802? Do they *really* know that number down to a single fraction of a degree? I'm skeptical and you should be, too.

Warming Alarmist

My confidence in the conclusion of these alarmist scientists is further weakened because I've been here before. For as long as I can remember the "experts"—many the very same people pushing global warming hysteria today—have been predicting one ecological disaster after another. In the 1970s and virtually every year afterwards, we were doomed—doomed!!!—to global cooling, global wetting, global drying, mass starvation, acid rain, an epidemic of heterosexual AIDS, Mad Cow and, just the other day, a deadly pandemic of Swine Flu. Alarmism seems to be a tactic employed by scientists to draw attention to their causes, garner major funding and make a name for themselves and hyped by a willing news (and publishing) media because hysteria sells.

Anti-scientific Responses

My trust in the conclusions of the alarmists is even further diminished by the unscientific methods the alarmists are using in their efforts. Not only are we now privy to leaked documents emailed back-and-forth between those at the head of the "climate change" research detailing the destruction of their work and their underhanded methods of preventing Freedom of Information laws to allow others to double-check their supposed findings, but the campaign to slander other scientists—those whose work sheds doubt on the alarmists' claims—reeks of the kind of cowardice shown by those who know they are lying. Slander is not a scientific practice. Dubbing anyone who challenges their hysterical campaign as being like Holocaust deniers is an ad hominem attack with no scientific merit. In fact, it is *anti*-scientific, a means to discredit the man rather than answering the opposing science.

Another of the alarmists' ad hominem attacks—that anyone who questions their conclusions has been bought off by "big oil" (as [former vice president and now environmentalist] Al Gore proclaimed in his testimony before Congress)—is not only a lie but a completely illogical claim. Whatever grant money a scientist may receive from the "evil" folks at Exxon/ Mobil, etc. is nothing next to the tens of millions of dollars pocketed by folks like Al Gore. If one believes that all questions can be answered by "following the money," then the scientist with a fifty-thousand dollar research grant from "big oil" (who must then weather the hate-mongering of the global warming establishment, put his job at risk and condemn both himself and everyone he knows and loves to a global catastrophe unequaled in human history) is not the guy to be questioning. If the "denier" is lying, he dies. If Al Gore is lying he gets to live into a ripe old age spending millions, jet-setting around the globe and showing off his Oscar and his Nobel Prize to the beautiful people in Hollywood and Cannes. If science is to be determined by who has the more obvious motive, it's pretty clear that the Al Gores are the ones who are lying.

Gore et al.'s Hypocrisy

And it sure doesn't do much to bring me to the alarmist's side to witness Mr. Gore (and his fellow "scientists") flying all over the world in private jets, caravanning with his entourage in gas-guzzling SUVs (leaving the motors running so that when they return the temperature will be in their "comfort zone") and spewing pollution from his mansion at rates many times that of the average citizen he and his ilk so disparage for their "consumption." If Mr. Gore (et al) truly believed that catastrophe was imminent, one would suspect he would attempt to lead by example, not luxuriate in his newly-gained and fabulous riches while screaming "the world will end tomnorrow!!!"

I also recognize as unscientific the creation of and adoration for Mr. Gore's movie *An Inconvenient Truth*. This film, produced by Laurie David (ex-wife of *Seinfeld* creator Larry David), is filled with "facts" well-known to be (and acknowledged as such even by scientists employed in the making of the movie) hyperbolic at best and often out-and-out lies. That this is "documentary"—created by a D student in earth science and a Hollywood leftist whose greatest prior accomplishment was marrying a very funny man—is the "educational" tool being used to promote hysteria speaks volumes about how little there is to be truthfully said. The fact that those who continue to promote this propaganda effort, fully aware of the half-truths and out-right lies, makes clear that science (i.e. truth) is not, to them, sacrosanct. When scientists recognize that they cannot use the science to prove their science then, well, it's probably not science.

Nor does the campaign to brainwash small children—frighten them—with a propaganda film do much to earn my confidence. Leave the children alone. When scientists recognize that they can't win the day with adults so they attack small children with fear-mongering, chances are good the science isn't.

Think global socialism and suddenly the Kyoto Protocols make sense.

An Unequal Remedy

And just as their "science" fills me with doubts and their methods increase my skepticism, so too does their proposed remedy. Under the Kyoto Protocol [an international treaty that seeks to limit greenhouse gas emissions] the most egregious polluters get to continue to pollute unabated while some of the most ecologically advanced nations face draconian punishment. If we were really as close to doom as the hysterics attempt to convince our children, *everyone* would be asked to sacrifice. Instead, it seems that the "remedy" being proposed is really nothing more than your usual Leftist efforts to redistribute wealth along the lines of an affirmative action program. Successful nations will be shackled, failed nations will be rewarded and, well, think global socialism and suddenly the Kyoto Protocols make sense.

And lo and behold, the very same folks who are screaming "the world will end tomorrow" and then destroying the evidence, pocketing millions, flying around the globe to pick up their rewards and honors are *exactly* the same people who support every other leftist, socialist, punish-the-successful/reward-the-failure policy.

No matter how you look at the issue—which is why the alarmists are so determined to never allow you to actually look at the issue—anyone who thinks must be skeptical of the claims of the hysterics. The science is new, its models based on utterly unverifiable numbers (i.e. the temperature in Guam in the year 8), the accuracy of its long-term predictions obviously impossible to know, its short-term predictions having utterly failed to come to be (e.g. that decade-and-a-half long hiatus in global warming.) The behaviors of the hysterical scientists are unscientific, the behavior of the hysteric's favorite celebrities contradictory to those someone who truly believed would be engaging in. If you follow the money it is almost entirely into the pockets of the hysterics while the proposed "remedy" does not seem to be those that would be proposed by people who believed the end is near. In fact, what the remedy *does* suggest—what the entire industry of the hysterics suggests—is that "manmade global warming" is a leftist farce being perpetrated by cynics who recognize there's riches to be had, along with power and fame.

The Scientific and Policy Debate About Global Warming Has Just Begun

Karin McQuillan

Karin McQuillan is a retired psychotherapist, author of mystery novels, and a frequent contributor of political articles to Ameri-can Thinker, *a daily Internet publication devoted to American policy issues.*

Global warming became a cause to save life on earth be-fore it had a chance to become good science. The belief that fossil fuel use is an emergency destroying our planet by CO_2 [carbon dioxide] emissions took the media and political arena by storm. The issue was politicized so quickly that the normal scientific process was stunted. We have never had a full, honest national debate on either the science or govern-ment policy issues.

Everyone "knows" that global warming is true. The public has no idea of the number of scientists—precisely one thou-sand at last count of a congressional committee—who believe that global warming is benign and natural, and that it ended in 1998. We have not been informed of the costs to our economy of discouraging fossil fuel development and promot-ing alternatives. The public need to know the choices being made on their behalf, and to have a say in the matter. We are constantly told that the scientific and policy debate on global warming is over. It has just begun.

What is never discussed is this: the theory of global warm-ing has catastrophic implications for our economy and na-tional security. Case in point: [President Barack] Obama's recent decision to block the Keystone pipeline in order to placate global warming advocates. Key Democrat supporters fear the use of oil more than they care about losing jobs or our dangerous dependence on the Mideast for oil. The president delayed the pipeline by fiat, and the general public has had no say. . . .

Storm cycles and long patterns of bad weather are entirely natural.

President Obama has spoken out passionately on the danger of developing oil and gas because of man-made global warming. "What we can be scientifically certain of is that our continued use of fossil fuels is pushing us to a point of no return. And unless we free ourselves from a dependence on these fossil fuels and chart a new course on energy in this country, we are condemning future generations to global catastrophe."

Obama calls for the debate to end. He cites hurricanes as proof: "dangerous weather patterns and devastating storms are abruptly putting an end to the long-running debate over whether or not climate change is real. Not only is it real—it's here, and its effects are giving rise to a frighteningly new global phenomenon: the man-made natural disaster."

Happily, our president is wrong. The worst hurricanes were in 1926, the second-worst in 1900. The world's top hurricane experts say that there is no evidence that global warming affects storms. There is no such thing as a man-made hurricane. Storm cycles and long patterns of bad weather are entirely natural. Yet this good news is suppressed by our politicized media. We hear only one side.

More and more scientists are revolting against the global warming consensus enforced by government funding, the academic establishment, and media misrepresentation. They are saying that solar cycles and the complex systems of cloud formation have much more influence on our climate, and account for historical periods of warming and cooling much more accurately than a straight line graph of industrialization, CO_2, and rising temperatures. They also point out that the rising temperatures that set off the global warming panic ended in 1998.

A Stalinist-Type Consensus

It takes a lot of courage. Scientists who report findings that contradict man-made global warming find their sources of funding cut, their jobs terminated, their careers stunted, and their reports blocked from important journals, and they are victimized by personal attacks. This is a consensus one associates with a Stalinist system, not science in the free world.

Here is how it has worked. The theory that entirely natural sun cycles best explain warming patterns emerged years ago, but the Danish scientists [according to an article by Lawrence Solomon in the *Financial Post*] "soon found themselves vilified, marginalized and starved of funding, despite their impeccable scientific credentials." Physicists at Europe's most prestigious CERN [European Organization for Nuclear Research] laboratory tried to test the solar theory in 1996, and they, too, found their project blocked. This fall, the top scientific journal *Nature* published the first experimental proof—by a team of 63 scientists at CERN—that the largest factor in global warming is the sun, not humans. But the director of CERN forbade the implications of the experiment to be explained to the public: "I have asked the colleagues to present the results clearly, but not to interpret them. That would go immediately into the highly political arena of the climate change debate."

As more and more scientific evidence is published that debunks global warming, the enforced consensus is ending. The Royal Society, Britain's premier scientific institution—whose previous president declared that "the debate on climate change is over"—"is being forced to review its statements on climate change after a rebellion by members who question mankind's contribution to rising temperatures. . . . The society has been accused by 43 of its Fellows of refusing to accept dissenting views on climate change and exaggerating the degree of certainty that man-made emissions are the main cause." Most of the rebels were retired, as one of them explained, "One of the reasons people like myself are willing to put our heads above the parapet is that our careers are not at risk from being labeled a denier or flat-Earther because we say the science is not settled. The bullying of people into silence has unfortunately been effective."

Dr. Giaever

In America, Dr. Ivar Giaever, a Nobel Prize–winner in physics, resigned in protest from the American Physical Society [APS] this fall [2011] because of the Society's policy statement: "The evidence is incontrovertible: global warming is occurring." Dr. Giaver:

> Incontrovertible is not a scientific word. Nothing is incontrovertible in science.

> In the APS it is ok to discuss whether the mass of the proton changes over time and how a multi-universe behaves, but the evidence of global warming is incontrovertible?

> The claim (how can you measure the average temperature of the whole earth for a whole year?) is that the temperature has changed from ~288.0 to ~288.8 degrees Kelvin in about 150 years, which (if true) means to me that the temperature has been amazingly stable, and both human health and happiness have definitely improved in this "warming" period.

In 2008, Prof. Giaever endorsed Barack Obama's candidacy, but he has since joined 100 scientists who wrote an open letter to Obama, declaring: "We maintain that the case for alarm regarding climate change is grossly overstated."

Do a Google search: you will find this letter reported in Britain and even India, but not in America.

Fifty-one thousand Canadian engineers, geologists, and geophysicists were recently polled by their professional organization. Sixty-eight percent of them disagree with the statement that "the debate on the scientific causes of recent climate change is settled." Only 26% attributed global warming to "human activity like burning fossil fuels." APEGGA's [Association of Professional Engineers, Geologists, and Geophysicists of Alberta] executive director Neil Windsor said, "We're not surprised at all. There is no clear consensus of scientists that we know of."

Computer models are not yet good enough to predict weather—we cannot scientifically predict global climate trends.

Dr. Joanne Simpson, one of the world's top weather scientists, expressed relief upon her retirement that she was finally free to speak "frankly" on global warming and announce that "as a scientist I remain skeptical." She says she remained silent for fear of personal attacks. Dr. Simpson was a pioneer in computer modeling and points out the obvious: computer models are not yet good enough to predict weather—we cannot scientifically predict global climate trends.

Dr. Fred Singer, first director of the U.S. Weather Satellite Service, and physicist Dr. Seitz, past president of the APS, of Rockefeller University and of the National Academy of Science, argue that the computer models are fed questionable data and assumptions that determine the answers on global warming that the scientists expect to see.

Recently we've had a perfect example of the enforced global warming consensus falling apart. Berkeley Professor [Richard] Muller did a media blitz with the findings of the latest analysis of all land temperature data, the BEST [Berkeley

Earth Surface Temperatures] study, that he claimed once and for all proved that the planet is warming. Predictably, the *Washington Post* proclaimed that the BEST study had "settled the climate change debate" and showed that anyone who remained a skeptic was committing a "cynical fraud."

But within a week, Muller's lead co-author, Professor [Judith] Curry, was interviewed in the British press (not reported in America), saying that the BEST data did the opposite: the global "temperature trend of the last decade is absolutely flat, with no increase at all—though the levels of carbon dioxide in the atmosphere have carried on rising relentlessly."

Unethical Claims

"This is nowhere near what the climate models were predicting," Prof Curry said. "Whatever it is that's going on here, it doesn't look like it's being dominated by CO_2." In fact, she added, in the wake of the unexpected global warming *standstill*, many climate scientists who had previously rejected sceptics' arguments were now taking them much more seriously. They were finally addressing questions such as the influence of clouds, natural temperature cycles and solar radiation—as they should have done, she said, a long time ago.

Other scientists jumped in, calling Muller's false claims to the media that BEST proved global warming "highly unethical." Professor Muller, confronted with dissent, caved and admitted that indeed, both ocean and land measurements show that global warming stopped increasing in 1998.

Media coverage on global warming has been criminally one-sided. The public doesn't know where the global warming theory came from in the first place. Answer: the U.N., not a scientific body. The threat of catastrophic warming was launched by the U.N. to promote international climate treaties that would transfer wealth from rich countries to developing countries. It was political from the beginning, with the conclusion assumed: the Intergovernmental Panel on Climate

Change (U.N. IPCC) was funded to report on how man was changing climate. Its scientific reports have been repeatedly corrected for misrepresentation and outright fraud.

Global warming regulations . . . will cost American consumers $300 to $400 billion a year, significantly raise energy prices, and destroy hundreds of thousands of jobs.

This is important. Global warming theory did not come from a breakthrough in scientific research that enabled us to understand our climate. We still don't understand global climate any more than we understand the human brain or how to cure cancer. The science of global climate is in its infancy.

Yet the U.N. IPCC reports drive American policy. The EPA [Environmental Protection Agency] broke federal law requiring independent analysis and used the U.N. IPCC reports in its "endangerment" finding that justifies extreme regulatory actions. Senator [James] Inhofe is apoplectic:

> Global warming regulations imposed by the Obama-EPA under the Clean Air Act will cost American consumers $300 to $400 billion a year, significantly raise energy prices, and destroy hundreds of thousands of jobs. This is not to mention the 'absurd result' that EPA will need to hire 230,000 additional employees and spend an additional $21 billion to implement its [greenhouse gas] regime.

Former top scientists at the U.N. IPCC are protesting publicly against falsification of global warming data and misleading media reports. Dr. John Everett, for example, was the lead researcher on Fisheries, Polar Regions, Oceans and Coastal Zones at the IPCC and a former National Oceanic and Atmospheric Administration (NOAA) senior manager, and he received an award while at NOAA for "accomplishments in assessing the impacts of climate change on global oceans and fisheries." Here is what he has to say on global warming:

It is time for a reality check. Warming is not a big deal and is not a bad thing. The oceans and coastal zones have been far warmer and colder than is projected in the present scenarios. . . . I would much rather have the present warm climate, and even further warming. . . . No one knows whether the Earth is going to keep warming, or since reaching a peak in 1998, we are at the start of a cooling cycle that will last several decades or more.

The Need for Solid Science

That is why we must hear from all the best scientists, not only those who say fossil fuel use is dangerous. It is very important that we honestly discuss whether this theory is true and, if so, what reasonable steps we can afford to take to mitigate warming. If the theory is not based on solid science, we are free to develop our fossil fuel wealth responsibly and swiftly.

Instead, federal policies are based on global warming fears. Obama has adopted the California model. The Global Warming Solutions Act of 2006 has shed a million jobs in that state. California now has almost 12% unemployment, ranking 50th in the nation.

Warming advocates persistently argue that we cannot afford to pause for a reality check.

The country could be following North Dakota, where oil development has led to a 3.5% unemployment rate, or Texas, which has created 40% of the jobs nationwide since the 2009 economic crash thanks to its robust energy sector. These are good jobs. An entry-level job on an oil rig pays $70,000 a year. A roughneck with a high school diploma earns $100,000 a year in Wyoming's Jonah Fields. Brazil's new offshore oil discoveries are predicted to create 2 million jobs there. We have almost three times more oil than Brazil.

When we treat oil and gas companies like pariahs, we threaten America's economic viability. For global warming alarmists who believe that man-made CO_2 threatens life on earth, no cost is too high to fight it. They avert their eyes from the human suffering of people without jobs, with diminished life savings, limited future prospects, and looming national bankruptcy.

This is not all about idealism. There are crasser reasons of money and power for wanting to close the debate. Billions of dollars in federal grants and subsidies are spent to fight global warming. The cover of fighting to save the planet gives the government unlimited powers to intrude into private business and our individual homes. The government can reach its long arm right into your shower and control how much hot water you are allowed to use. In the words of MIT [Massachusetts Institute of Technology] atmospheric scientist Dr. [Richard] Lindzen, "[c]ontrolling carbon is kind of a bureaucrat's dream. If you control carbon, you control life."

Warming advocates persistently argue that we cannot afford to pause for a reality check; we must not ignore the *possibility* that global warming theory might be true. Limiting fossil fuels and promoting green energy are presented as a benign, a "why not be on the safe side," commonsense approach.

There is a lot of emotion and little common sense in this argument. If a diagnosis is based on a shaky and partly fraudulent theory, ignores much more convincing evidence, and has terrible negative side effects, you don't perform major surgery. We do not have to run around like Chicken Little on the off-chance that the sky may be falling.

There has been a high economic cost to limiting our oil and gas wealth, with much human anguish because of government-imposed economic contraction. Responsible government policy requires honest media coverage, unfettered scientific inquiry, and robust political debate. Our country cannot afford the costs of foolish energy policy based on politicized science and fear.

Scientists Who Deny Global Warming Rely on Falsehoods and Out-of-Date Research

Joe Romm

Joe Romm is a physicist, a senior fellow at the Center for American Progress, and the editor of Climate Progress, *a blog about climate change. He also served in the federal government as acting assistant secretary of energy for energy efficiency and renewable energy in 1997.*

A lot of folks have asked me to debunk the recent anti-truthful *Wall Street Journal* [*WSJ*] article with the counterfactual headline, "No Need to Panic About Global Warming." I'll combine my debunking with the rapidly growing list of debunkings from scientists and others. And I'll update this as new debunkings come in.

That the *WSJ* would publish an amateurish collection of falsehoods and half truths is no surprise. The entire global [media mogul Rupert] Murdoch enterprise is designed to advance the pollutocrat do-nothing agenda. As National Academy of Sciences member Peter Gleick explains in his evisceration of the piece, "Remarkable Editorial Bias on Climate Science at the *Wall Street Journal*":

> But the most amazing and telling evidence of the bias of the *Wall Street Journal* in this field is the fact that 255 members of the United States National Academy of Sciences [NAS] wrote a comparable (but scientifically accurate) essay on the realities of climate change and on the need for improved and serious public debate around the issue, offered it to the

Wall Street Journal, and were turned down. The National Academy of Sciences is the nation's pre-eminent independent scientific organization. Its members are among the most respected in the world in their fields. Yet the *Journal* wouldn't publish this letter, from more than 15 times as many top scientists. Instead they chose to publish an error-filled and misleading piece on climate because some so-called experts aligned with their bias signed it. This may be good politics for them, but it is bad science and it is bad for the nation.

Science magazine—perhaps the nation's most important journal on scientific issues—published the letter from the NAS members after the *Journal* turned it down.

The last 10 years were easily the hottest on record.

A tad more surprising is that 16 admittedly non-leading scientists would choose to soil their reputations by stringing together a collection of long-debunked falsehoods. What is surprising is that these falsehoods are more easily debunked than the typical disinformer clap-trap because they are so out-of-date!

Guys, if you're going to push disinformation, you have to do better than this:

> Perhaps the most inconvenient fact is the lack of global warming for well over 10 years now. This is known to the warming establishment, as one can see from the 2009 "Climategate" email of climate scientist Kevin Trenberth: "The fact is that we can't account for the lack of warming at the moment and it is a travesty that we can't". . . .

> The lack of warming for more than a decade—indeed, the smaller-than-predicted warming over the 22 years since the U.N.'s Intergovernmental Panel on Climate Change (IPCC) began issuing projections—suggests that computer models have greatly exaggerated how much warming additional CO_2 can cause.

Well, . . . the last 10 years were easily the hottest on record. As the Union of Concerned Scientists' debunking notes, "2011 was the 35th year in a row in which global temperatures were above the historical average and 2010 and 2005 were the warmest years on record." Doh!

And apparently these guys missed the news that last year's Koch-Funded and Skeptic-Led Study Finds Recent Warming "On the High End" and Speeding Up. The Berkeley Earth Surface Temperature Study (BEST) concluded:

> . . . we find that the global land mean temperature has increased by 0.911 ± 0.042 C since the 1950s . . . our analysis suggests a degree of global land-surface warming during the anthropogenic era that is consistent with prior work (e.g. NOAA [National Oceanic and Atmospheric Administration]) but on the *high end* of the existing range of reconstruction.

Double Doh!

Debunked Scientists

Then again, what do you expect from a list of 16 scientists that include:

- Richard Lindzen, one of the most debunked climate scientists in the world.

- William Happer, physicist, Chairman of the Board of a leading disinformer think-tank George Marshall Institute, heavily funded by Exxon Mobil and other anti-science funders.

- Roger Cohen, Former manager for Strategic Planning and Programs ExxonMobil Corporation, now a George Marshall Institute 'expert'.

- Harrison H. Schmitt, geologist and astronaut, who believes enviros and climate scientists like [John] Holdren are communists.

This gang that couldn't shoot straight assert "it is likely that more CO_2 and the modest warming that may come with it will be an overall benefit to the planet." In fact, as Fatih Birol, the chief economist for the International Energy Agency explained last year [2011], the world is on pace for 11°F warming, and "Even School Children Know This Will Have Catastrophic Implications for All of Us."

There are all other kinds of signs aside from global mean temperatures—including melting of Arctic sea ice and rising sea levels and a lot of other indicators—that global warming is continuing.

Yes, even school children know more than these guys!

They utterly misrepresent the work of serious climatologists like Kevin Trenberth. Anybody who is actually paying attention to real science knows Trenberth explained 2 years ago that the way the disinformers were quoting him was nonsense, and they know recent analysis has done a good job of identifying where the "missing" warming went—the deep oceans. Let's go through this one more time.

As Trenberth explained back in 2009, we have a vast amount of evidence that "global warming is continuing":

> But Trenberth, who acknowledged the e-mail is genuine, says bloggers are missing the point he's making in the e-mail by not reading the article cited in it. That article—An Imperative for Climate Change Planning—actually says that global warming is continuing, despite random temperature variations that would seem to suggest otherwise.

> "It says we don't have an observing system adequate to track it, but there are all other kinds of signs aside from global mean temperatures—including melting of Arctic sea ice and rising sea levels and a lot of other indicators—that global warming is continuing," he says.

In the paper, Trenberth posited the very recent surface temperature data might not be keeping up with the other data showing global warming because of a variety of reasons, most significantly "Was it because the heat was buried in the ocean and sequestered, perhaps well below the surface?" The answer to that appears to be "yes."

The key point from recent observation is that whatever slight slowing in global warming some groups may have observed in the past decade, it was primarily in the surface temperature data set. The oceans kept warming. . . .

The Bali Climate Declaration

It is worth adding that Trenberth signed the Must Read Bali Climate Declaration by Leading Scientists, which opens:

> The 2007 IPCC report, compiled by several hundred climate scientists, has unequivocally concluded that our climate is warming rapidly, and that we are now at least 90% certain that this is mostly due to human activities. The amount of carbon dioxide in our atmosphere now far exceeds the natural range of the past 650,000 years, and it is rising very quickly due to human activity. If this trend is not halted soon, many millions of people will be at risk from extreme events such as heat waves, drought, floods and storms, our coasts and cities will be threatened by rising sea levels, and many ecosystems, plants and animal species will be in serious danger of extinction.

One can only dream that we lived in a world where that important declaration by more than 200 of the world's leading climate scientists would get more attention than either stolen emails or the silly sixteen.

The thing about these 16 scientists, the overwhelming majority of whom have no background whatsoever in climate science, is that because they don't know the scientific literature, they are forced to cling to out-of-date claptrap:

In 2003, Dr. Chris de Freitas, the editor of the journal *Climate Research*, dared to publish a peer-reviewed article with the politically incorrect (but factually correct) conclusion that the recent warming is not unusual in the context of climate changes over the past thousand years.

The last decades of the past millennium are characterized again by warm temperatures that seem to be unprecedented.

A nine-year-old paper? Really guys? If you want to know about de Freitas, DeSmogBlog has a great piece, "Skeptics Prefer Pal Review Over Peer Review: Chris de Freitas, Pat Michaels And Their Pals, 1997–2003."

But the key point is that in the past 9 years, there has been a National Academy of Sciences review of the literature and over a dozen independent studies making clear that "Recent global warming is unprecedented in magnitude and speed and cause." Here are a few:

- *GRL*: "We conclude that the 20th century warming of the incoming intermediate North Atlantic water has had no equivalent during the last thousand years."

- *JGR*: "The last decades of the past millennium are characterized again by warm temperatures that seem to be unprecedented in the context of the last 1600 years."

- Unprecedented warming in Lake Tanganyika and its impact on humanity (2010)

- Human-caused Arctic warming overtakes 2,000 years of natural cooling, "seminal" study finds (2009):

- Sorry disinformers, hockey stick gets longer, stronger: Earth hotter now than in past 2,000 years (2008)

- Arctic Sea Ice Hockey Stick: Melt Unprecedented in Last 1,450 Years (2011)

The entire op-ed is just a laughable collection of out of date and debunked disinformer talking points.

A Do-Nothing Agenda

Or, rather, it would be laughable if it weren't for the fact that the Murdoch outlet is using these 16 scientists to help push its do-nothing agenda. Here is the key argument:

> The fact is that CO_2 is not a pollutant. CO_2 is a colorless and odorless gas, exhaled at high concentrations by each of us, and a key component of the biosphere's life cycle. Plants do so much better with more CO_2 that greenhouse operators often increase the CO_2 concentrations by factors of three or four to get better growth. This is no surprise since plants and animals evolved when CO_2 concentrations were about 10 times larger than they are today. Better plant varieties, chemical fertilizers and agricultural management contributed to the great increase in agricultural yields of the past century, but part of the increase almost certainly came from additional CO_2 in the atmosphere. . . .
>
> A recent study of a wide variety of policy options by Yale economist William Nordhaus showed that nearly the highest benefit-to-cost ratio is achieved for a policy that allows *50 more years of economic growth unimpeded by greenhouse gas controls.* . . . And it is likely that more CO_2 and the modest warming that may come with it will be an overall benefit to the planet.

In short, let's do nothing and it'll probably all work out for the best. . . .

In fact, this perspective has already been quite well debunked in the literature. First off, we now know that the totality of impacts of global warming—warming, acidification, extreme weather, Dust-Bowlification—is already showing evidence of harm to the biosphere, biodiversity, and agriculture in particular:

- Oxfam: Extreme Weather Has Helped Push Tens of Millions into "Hunger and Poverty" in "Grim Foretaste" of Warmed World.

- Climate Story of the Year: Warming-Driven Drought and Extreme Weather Emerge as Key Threat to Global Food Security

- NCAR [National Center for Atmospheric Research] analysis warns we risk multiple, devastating global droughts even on moderate emissions path

---

Rising fossil energy use will lead to irreversible and potentially catastrophic climate change.

Second, the only way we could have modest warming is if we acted aggressively to reduce greenhouse gas emissions starting now. Ironically, or, rather, tragically, the one way to be absolutely certain of high levels of warming and catastrophic impacts is to do nothing for the next several decades, which is clearly what these 16 scientists are promoting. A review of 50 recent studies makes that clear—see "An Illustrated Guide to the Science of Global Warming Impacts: How We Know Inaction Is the Gravest Threat Humanity Faces." . . .

Rather than quoting one economist, Nordhaus, we should listen to the traditionally staid and conservative International Energy Agency in its recent IEA's 2011 World Energy Outlook [WEO]:

> "On planned policies, rising fossil energy use will lead to irreversible and potentially catastrophic climate change". . . .

> "Delaying action is a false economy: for every $1 of investment in cleaner technology that is avoided in the power sector before 2020, an additional $4.30 would need to be spent after 2020 to compensate for the increased emissions."

I started by saying this piece had a counterfactual headline, "No Need to Panic About Global Warming."

Panic is a sudden sensation of fear which is so strong as to dominate or prevent reason and logical thinking. . . .

It is the authors of the *WSJ* piece who are panicked because they have allowed their fear of climate action to "dominate or prevent reason and logical thinking." They have abandoned science. Climate scientists and other climate realists like the IEA are not urging panic—quite the opposite, we are urging a reasoned and logical science-based policy response.

The tragedy is that if we listen to Rupert Murdoch's media outlets and the handful of scientists willing to push anti-scientific nonsense, if we keep taking no serious action to reduce greenhouse gas emissions, then we make it far more likely that future generations will in fact panic, when they wake up sometime in the 2020s and realize how dire the situation is but how the disinformers have all but ended the possibility for averting catastrophe.

Global Warming Skeptics Are Motivated by Ideology, Not Science

Phil Plait

Phil Plait is an astronomer, lecturer, writer, and author who worked on the Hubble Space Telescope and now writes about science topics.

Before I say anything else in this post, I will start off right away and say that the results I'll be discussing here have not yet been published in a peer-reviewed journal. Because of that, the results need to be taken with a grain of salt. However, due to the nature of the study's foundation and funders, which I will get to in a moment, the results are most definitely newsworthy.

The study is called the Berkeley Earth Project (BEP), and what they found was stated simply and beautifully in their own two-page summary:

> Global warming is real, according to a major study released today. Despite issues raised by climate change skeptics, the Berkeley Earth Surface Temperature study finds reliable evidence of a rise in the average world land temperature of approximately 1° C since the mid-1950s.

Wow. Of course, I would change one word in there. Can you guess what it is? The answer is below.

Now, we've known this for a while. Study after study has shown that the Earth is warming, that the past decade has been the hottest on record, and that the rise in temperature has been about a degree. So what's the big deal here?

The big deal is that this was an *independent* team of researchers who conducted the study (including, interestingly, Saul Perlmutter, who just won the Nobel Prize for co-discovering the acceleration of the expansion of the Universe, and knows a thing or two about data analysis), and whose funding was overwhelmingly donated by the private sector and not from any government. The study was initiated by Berkeley physicist Richard Muller, who was concerned that government researchers weren't being as open as possible with their methods. He gathered together a team of scientists, and they used data from 39,000 temperature stations around the world, far more than the previous studies. They have put all their data and methodology online for anyone to investigate.

And if you're wondering who these private groups were, they're listed on the BEP website. The largest single donor? Why, it's *the Koch brothers*, über-conservatives who have pumped millions of dollars into climate change denial. I find that . . . interesting.

Anyone claiming that climate scientists are alarmists only trying to protect their grant money will have to think about *that* one for a while.

Getting Warmer

So what did the scientists working on BEP find? Well, first, and perhaps most importantly, their results agree in large part with what has been found by other groups: temperatures over land are rising, and that rise took a sudden leap up a few decades ago. . . . In this case, they took the values from 1950 to 1980 and used that as a baseline—this is pretty standard practice in climate studies. Four different studies are plotted, including the BEP results. . . . All of them show a big rise, and the BEP results agree closely with (or are even greater than) the results from NASA's [National Aeronautics and Space Administration's] Goddard Institute for Space Studies [GISS].

Scientists at NASA/GISS were attacked heavily during "climategate" [a 2009 scandal revealing that climate scientists were falsifying data] for (at best) being misleading with their results. As you can see, that turned out to be wrong all along. As we knew all along, in fact.

What [the Berkeley study] found is that if you take enough data, the warming trends show up even if an individual result may be low quality.

There were other very interesting results as well. For example, a favorite target for attack were the temperature readings from many of the monitoring stations around the country; the claim was that they suffer from urban heat effect, that is, they are near cities and therefore would be anomalously warm. The new study shows this is *not* a factor in the average land temperature rise; while some stations do appear warmer from this, they represent a tiny fraction of the total number of monitoring stations.

Not only that, stations that were ranked as "poor" in a survey done by Anthony Watts wound up showing the same warming results as those he marked as "OK." What BEP found is that if you take enough data, the warming trends show up even if an individual result may be low quality.

The BEP reports are fascinating reading, and I wholeheartedly suggest you take a look. That's why they've been made public. Again, I'll note that these have not been peer-reviewed, so it'll be interesting to see the reactions to the public data and methods. But given the scientists involved, and Muller's own admission that he didn't like the way the previous science had been done and so he wanted to go over all this himself, I suspect this report will withstand the scrutiny.

In the report summary, BEP Executive Director Elizabeth Muller says she hopes the results "will help cool the debate over global warming by addressing many of the valid concerns of the skeptics in a clear and rigorous way."

I strongly suspect they won't. I do like her use of the word "valid"; so many of the attacks we've seen have not been so. There have been legitimate doubts raised scientifically, of course, about various factors that go into the results we've seen over the years. It looks like BEP now has those covered.

Still, her thoughts are mirrored by Bob Ward, the policy and communications director for the Grantham Institute for Climate Change and the Environment, who said:

> So-called 'sceptics' should now drop their thoroughly discredited claims that the increase in global average temperature could be attributed to the impact of growing cities. [...] It is now time for an apology from all those, including US presidential hopeful Rick Perry, who have made false claims that the evidence for global warming has been faked by climate scientists.

This, of course, will never happen.

That's because of that one word I said I would change in the report's summary paragraph. That word is "skeptic," and in far too many cases it should be changed to "denier."

That includes a lot of other government officials who seem to overwhelmingly have an "R" [Republican] listed as their party affiliation.

Eternal Vigilance

I know this new study won't sway climate change deniers. It can't, *because nothing can*. The reason for that is simple: This isn't about the science. If it were, the conversation would have been over years ago. Instead, it goes on, because it's about ideology, not facts.

It's nice to see the previous scientific studies bolstered by this independent one, and there's more good news in that the American public now seems to understand that global warming is indeed real. And it was nice to see BEP lead scientist Richard Muller saying, at the bottom of a BBC article on this, that these results support the idea that it's humans causing the rise in temperatures.

But, as I have been saying all along, there will *never* be a "crossing the finish line" moment. Whether it's the Moon Hoax, or vaccines causing autism, or psychics talking to the dead, or climate change denial, this will be a continuing fight. It's tiring, I know. But we should remember the words of Andrew Jackson:

". . . Eternal vigilance by the people is the price of liberty, and that you must pay the price if you wish to secure the blessing."

Skeptics Are Free-Market Fundamentalists Who Seek to Undermine Scientific Evidence of Global Warming

Naomi Oreskes and Erik M. Conway

Naomi Oreskes is a professor of history and science at the University of California, San Diego. Erik M. Conway is the author of several books. Oreskes and Conway coauthored the 2011 book Merchants of Doubt: How a Handful of Scientists Obscured the Truth on Issues from Tobacco Smoke to Global Warming.

In recent months, a group called the Cooler Heads Coalition—a creation of the Washington-based [think-tank] Competitive Enterprise Institute (CEI)—has fostered a public image of climate science as a criminal conspiracy. The CEI itself has accused NASA [National Aeronautic and Space Administration] the largest funder of climate science, of faking important climate data sets. In February [2010], U.S. Sen. James Inhofe of Oklahoma, whose positions are frequently cited and promoted by CEI, called for a criminal investigation of 17 climate scientists from a variety of institutions for allegedly falsifying or distorting data used in taxpayer-funded research.

The recent shift in the community of global warming deniers from merely attacking mainstream climate scientists to alleging their involvement in criminal activity is an unsurprising but alarming development in the long campaign to discredit the established scientific fact that burning fossil fuels is causing the world to warm. This latest escalation fits seam-

Naomi Oreskes and Erik M. Conway, "Global Warming Deniers and Their Proven Strategy of Doubt," Environment 360, June 10, 2010, e360.yale.edu. Copyright © 2010 by Ayesha Pande Literary on behalf of the authors. All rights reserved. Reproduced by permission.

lessly into a decades-old pattern of attempts to deny the reality of environmental ills—smoking, acid rain, ozone depletion, and global warming. Similar or even identical claims have been promoted for decades by other free-market thinktanks, including the American Enterprise Institute, the Cato Institute, the Heartland Institute, and, most persistently, the George C. Marshall Institute. These think tanks all have two things in common: They promote free-market solutions to environmental problems, and all have long been active in challenging the scientific evidence of those problems.

There has been a stepped-up effort on a broad front to belittle the overwhelming evidence of human-caused global warming.

In researching a book on global warming deniers, we often felt demoralized by the efficacy of doubt-mongering tactics and depressed that the American public had been repeatedly fooled by the same strategy and tactics. On the other hand, we felt cautiously optimistic because disputes over other issues—tobacco smoking, acid rain, second-hand smoke, and the ozone hole—ended with the scientific evidence prevailing, and with regulation that (however delayed or weakened) addressed the problem.

Global warming was the great unfinished story, but with the mainstream media and many politicians acknowledging the reality of global warming in recent years, it seemed that there was real progress. "The debate is over," California Gov. Arnold Schwarzenegger declared in 2005. "We know the science. We see the threat posed by changes in our climate."

Now it seems that progress has been reversed. In recent months, as the U.S. Senate prepared to consider climate and energy legislation, there has been a stepped-up effort on a broad front to belittle the overwhelming evidence of human-caused global warming. As they did with smoking and acid rain, the so-called global warming skeptics have had one over-riding goal: to sow doubt in the public's mind and head off government regulation.

In the case of global warming, there is strong evidence that this contrarian campaign is enjoying success, with recent polls showing that more than half of Americans are not particularly worried about the issue and that fully 40 percent believe there is major disagreement among scientists about whether climate change is even occurring. This confusion is no doubt due, at least in part, to the persistent campaigns of obfuscation by the Competitive Enterprise Institute and other global warming deniers who use right-wing talk radio, the Internet, and television programs such as Fox News to propagate their message of doubt.

Fighting Science

The story begins with the tobacco companies' long-running effort to cast doubt on the links between cigarette smoking and human health effects, including lung cancer. One of the scientists the tobacco industry recruited to this cause was Frederick Seitz. Seitz was a distinguished solid-state physicist, who believed strongly in the role of science and technology in defending the United States during the Cold War. In the late 1950s and 1960s he rose to high levels in national science policy, serving, among other positions, as president of the U.S. National Academy of Sciences.

However, in 1979, toward the end of his career, he took a new job: running a $45 million program for R.J. Reynolds Tobacco to support scientific research to defend the "product"—that is to say, tobacco—long after scientists and physicians had come to virtually unanimous agreement on the overwhelming harm that it caused.

In the words of one industry document, Seitz's program was to develop "an extensive body of scientifically, well-grounded data useful in defending the industry against attacks." The goal was to fight science with science—or at least with the gaps and uncertainties in existing science, and with scientific research that could be used to deflect attention from the main event. Like the magician who waves his right hand to distract attention from what he is doing with his left, the tobacco industry would fund distracting research, such as studies on the dietary causes of atherosclerosis and the role of patients' psychological attitudes on the progression of disease.

The George C. Marshall Institute

In 1984, Seitz took up another cause, joining with two other prominent physicists, William Nierenberg and Robert Jastrow—both also long active in space and weapons programs—to found the George C. Marshall Institute. They created the institute to defend President [Ronald] Reagan's Strategic Defense Initiative (SDI) from attacks by the mainstream physics community. The Marshall Institute drew its funding from a handful of conservative political foundations, and it defended SDI by loud claims of Soviet military superiority, claims that were found only a few years later—when the USSR [Soviet Union] disintegrated and the Cold War ended—to have been exaggerated, at best. However, although the Soviet threat was gone and the Cold War was won, the institute didn't go out of business. Instead, it found a new enemy: environmentalists.

In the early 1980s, Nierenberg had chaired a major National Academy of Sciences review of global warming. Scientists had formed a consensus in the late 1970s that global warming was likely to result from increasing greenhouse gases released by burning fossil fuels, and that this would have serious consequences: glaciers and polar ice sheets would melt, causing sea levels to rise and inundating coastlines and major port cities; deserts would expand, reducing food production; and rapid habitat change could lead to serious biodiversity loss. But as chairman of the panel, Nierenberg rejected the conclusions of his fellow physical scientists and recruited several economists who argued that, rather than trying to prevent climate change, we should simply wait and see what happened and then adapt as events unfolded. If adaptation proved impossible, humans could always migrate, Nierenberg concluded, ignoring the overwhelming historical evidence of the widespread human suffering that has typically accompanied mass migration.

Nierenberg also worked behind the scenes . . . to soften the conclusions of the [acid rain] report . . . and to make them seem more ambiguous than they had originally been.

Nierenberg also joined with another physicist, S. Fred Singer, to undermine regulatory action on sulfur dioxide, the principal cause of acid rain. In response to two National Academy reports suggesting that acid rain was real and serious, and its primary causes known, President Reagan commissioned an independent peer review of the existing scientific evidence. Most of the panel members *were*, actually, independent, and agreed with the National Academy that regulatory action to control sulfur emissions was warranted. However, Nierenberg and Singer worked to challenge that conclusion, adding a policy-oriented appendix by Singer—which was not approved by the entire panel—that first advocated free-market approaches to controlling pollution, and then concluded (but without a real quantitative analysis) that the cost of reducing acid rain would very likely exceed the benefits. Nierenberg also worked behind the scenes with White House Science Advisor George Keyworth to soften the conclusions of the report's executive summary and to make them seem more ambiguous than they had originally been. (Something Nierenberg would later accuse climate scientists of doing—only in the reverse.)

Despite these machinations, the acid rain report was still stronger than the Reagan White House wanted, and the administration delayed releasing it until *after* Congress had defeated pending acid rain legislation. Several congresspersons later stated that had the peer review report been available when the vote was taken, it might well have gone the other way.

It took several more years before the administration of George H.W. Bush implemented an acid rain reduction program organized around a cap-and-trade system. In one sense, this program has worked, reducing acid deposition in the Northeast by more than 50 percent, and—contrary to Singer's claims—at *one-tenth* of the projected cost. But it was also too little, too late. Continued work by ecologists such as Gene Likens shows that Northeastern forests are still dying.

Similar attacks were launched against the scientific evidence of the ozone hole, of second-hand smoke, and of the harms of DDT.

Denying Global Warming Science

In the late 1980s, the Marshall Institute turned to the denial of global warming. As scientific evidence emerged that warming was not only *going* to happen, but was perhaps *already* happening, the institute's attacks became stronger and more unprincipled. These "contrarians"—because their positions were contrary to the majority scientific view—began taking evidence out of context, cherry-picking data, and misrepresenting what was actually being published in the scientific literature. For example, they distributed a "white paper" in 1989 falsely claiming that a review from NASA climate scientist James Hansen showed that recent warming was largely due to increased solar activity.

When confronted with incontrovertible evidence that their arguments and cherry-picked facts were incorrect, the deniers refused to correct their mistakes and continued to spread the same misinformation. Indeed, as the science strengthened, and the evidence of the human fingerprint on the climate system began to strongly emerge, the contrarian attacks became more virulent, more unprincipled, and more personal.

In 1995, the Intergovernmental Panel on Climate Change [IPCC] prepared to release its second assessment report, which would declare that the human effect on climate was now "discernible." That same year, a fossil-fuel-industry-funded group called the Global Climate Coalition accused Benjamin Santer, a scientist at the Lawrence Livermore National Laboratory and lead author of a key IPCC chapter, of committing "scientific cleansing"—that is, of removing mention of uncertainties in the chapter to make global warming appear more certain than it was. The men of the Marshall Institute then splashed that accusation onto the op-ed pages of the *Wall Street Journal*. Investigations found nothing untoward had happened. All Santer had done was include new findings on global warming suggested by fellow scientists during the peer-review process and to clarify language that was also suggested in the peer review process. Various colleagues and IPCC officials defended Santer and tried to set the record straight, but it didn't matter. Indeed, in 2007, Fred Singer repeated the charges in a new book, and they continue to be repeated on the Internet today.

If all this sounds familiar, it should. Similar attacks were launched against the scientific evidence of the ozone hole, of second-hand smoke, and of the harms of DDT [a toxic pesticide]. As one tobacco executive put it in 1969, "Doubt is our product, since it is the best means of competing with the 'body of fact' that exists in the minds of the general public." Casting doubt about climate science is simply part of the effort to prevent regulation of fossil fuels. The point of merchandising doubt was, and remains, the prevention of government regulation.

These opponents of science are free-market fundamentalists, unwilling to accept that global warming and many other pollution-induced ills are market failures, and that government action of some kind will be needed to address it. Market fundamentalists believe that free markets are the solution to social problems and government intervention can only do harm. The reality, however, amply demonstrated by experience, is that pollution is external to the market system—there's no cost to dumping waste into the air and water. And as Lord Nicholas Stern has recently noted, global warming is the biggest market failure of them all. But this is yet another truth that the free market fundamentalists prefer to ignore.

Meanwhile, the contrarians' campaigns continue, and with significant success: Many Americans accept the deniers' allegations as true, or at least are confused by them, and therefore do not know what to think or whom to trust. Science has been effectively undermined, which has eroded public support for the decisive action needed to avoid the worst effects of global warming.

The Fossil Fuel Industry Is Funding Global-Warming Denial

Bill McKibben

Bill McKibben is the founder of the global climate campaign 350.org and the author of numerous books on the environment, including the 2011 Earth: Making a Life on a Tough New Planet.

If we could see the world with a particularly illuminating set of spectacles, one of its most prominent features at the moment would be a giant carbon bubble, whose bursting someday will make the housing bubble of 2007 look like a lark. As yet—as we shall see—it's unfortunately largely invisible to us.

In compensation, though, we have some truly beautiful images made possible by new technology. Last month [January 2012], for instance, NASA [National Aeronautics and Space Administration] updated the most iconic photograph in our civilization's gallery: "Blue Marble," originally taken from Apollo 17 in 1972. The spectacular new high-def image shows a picture of the Americas on January 4th [2012], a good day for snapping photos because there weren't many clouds.

It was also a good day because of the striking way it could demonstrate to us just how much the planet has changed in 40 years. As Jeff Masters, the web's most widely read meteorologist, explains, "The U.S. and Canada are virtually snow-free and cloud-free, which is extremely rare for a January day. The lack of snow in the mountains of the Western U.S. is particularly unusual. I doubt one could find a January day this cloud-free with so little snow on the ground throughout the entire satellite record, going back to the early 1960s."

In fact, it's likely that the week that photo was taken will prove [to be] "the driest first week in recorded U.S. history." Indeed, it followed on 2011, which showed the greatest weather extremes in our history—56% of the country was either in drought or flood, which was no surprise since "climate change science predicts wet areas will tend to get wetter and dry areas will tend to get drier." Indeed, the nation suffered 14 weather disasters each causing $1 billion or more in damage last year. (The old record was nine.) Masters again: "Watching the weather over the past two years has been like watching a famous baseball hitter on steroids."

Denying the Climate Change Problem

In the face of such data—statistics that you can duplicate for almost every region of the planet—you'd think we'd already be in an all-out effort to do something about climate change. Instead, we're witnessing an all-out effort to . . . deny there's a problem.

Our GOP [Republican] presidential candidates are working hard to make sure no one thinks they'd appease chemistry and physics. At the last Republican debate in Florida, Rick Santorum insisted that he should be the nominee because he'd caught on earlier than Newt [Gingrich] or Mitt [Romney] to the global warming "hoax."

Most of the media pays remarkably little attention to what's happening. Coverage of global warming has dipped 40% over the last two years. When, say, there's a rare outbreak of January tornadoes, TV anchors politely discuss "extreme weather," but climate change is the disaster that dare not speak its name.

And when they do break their silence, some of our elite organs are happy to indulge in outright denial. Last month, for instance, the *Wall Street Journal* published an op-ed by "16 scientists and engineers" headlined "No Need to Panic About Global Warming." The article was easily debunked. It was nothing but a mash-up of long-since-disproved arguments by people who turned out mostly not to be climate scientists at all, quoting other scientists who immediately said their actual work showed just the opposite.

The giant energy companies are making so much money right now that they can't stop gorging themselves.

It's no secret where this denialism comes from: the fossil fuel industry pays for it. (Of the 16 authors of the *Journal* article, for instance, five had had ties to Exxon.) Writers from Ross Gelbspan to Naomi Oreskes have made this case with such overwhelming power that no one even really tries denying it any more. The open question is *why* the industry persists in denial in the face of an endless body of fact showing climate change is the greatest danger we've ever faced.

Why doesn't it fold the way the tobacco industry eventually did? Why doesn't it invest its riches in things like solar panels and so profit handsomely from the next generation of energy? As it happens, the answer is more interesting than you might think.

Part of it's simple enough: the giant energy companies are making so much money right now that they can't stop gorging themselves. ExxonMobil, year after year, pulls in more money than any company in history. Chevron's not far behind. Everyone in the business is swimming in money.

Still, they could theoretically invest all that cash in new clean technology or research and development for the same. As it happens, though, they've got a deeper problem, one that's become clear only in the last few years. Put briefly: *their value is largely based on fossil-fuel reserves that won't be burned if we ever take global warming seriously.*

When I talked about a carbon bubble at the beginning of this essay, this is what I meant. Here are some of the relevant numbers, courtesy of the Capital Institute: we're already seeing widespread climate disruption, but if we want to avoid utter, civilization-shaking disaster, many scientists have pointed to a two-degree rise in global temperatures as the most we could possibly deal with.

If we spew 565 gigatons more carbon into the atmosphere, we'll quite possibly go right past that reddest of red lines. But the oil companies, private and state-owned, have current reserves on the books equivalent to 2,795 gigatons—five times more than we can ever safely burn. It has to stay in the ground.

Put another way, in ecological terms it would be extremely prudent to *write off $20 trillion worth* of those reserves. In economic terms, of course, it would be a disaster, first and foremost for shareholders and executives of companies like ExxonMobil (and people in places like Venezuela).

A Looming Carbon Bubble

If you run an oil company, this sort of write-off is the disastrous future staring you in the face as soon as climate change is taken as seriously as it should be, and that's far scarier than drought and flood. It's why you'll do anything—including fund an endless campaign of lies—to avoid coming to terms with its reality. So instead, we simply charge ahead. To take just one example, last month the boss of the U.S. Chamber of Commerce, Thomas Donohue, called for burning all the country's newly discovered coal, gas, and oil—believed to be 1,800 gigatons worth of carbon from our nation alone.

What he and the rest of the energy-industrial elite are denying, in other words, is that the business models at the center of our economy are in the deepest possible conflict with physics and chemistry. The carbon bubble that looms over our world needs to be deflated soon. As with our fiscal crisis, failure to do so will cause enormous pain—pain, in fact, almost beyond imagining. After all, if you think banks are too big to fail, consider the climate as a whole and imagine the nature of the bailout that would face us when that bubble finally bursts.

Unfortunately, it won't burst by itself—not in time, anyway. The fossil-fuel companies, with their heavily funded denialism and their record campaign contributions, have been able to keep at bay even the tamest efforts at reining in carbon emissions. With each passing day, they're leveraging us deeper into an unpayable carbon debt—and with each passing day, they're raking in unimaginable returns. ExxonMobil last week reported its 2011 profits at $41 billion, the second highest of all time. Do you wonder who owns the record? That would be ExxonMobil in 2008 at $45 billion.

Telling the truth about climate change would require pulling away the biggest punchbowl in history, right when the party is in full swing. That's why the fight is so pitched. That's why those of us battling for the future need to raise our game. And it's why that view from the satellites, however beautiful from a distance, is likely to become ever harder to recognize as our home planet.

Conservative Republicans Are in Denial About Global-Warming Science

Michael Stafford

Michael Stafford is an author; an attorney in Wilmington, Delaware; and a former Republican Party officer.

I'm a "climate change convert." Like many of my fellow conservatives, I was traditionally skeptical of the science supporting the anthropogenic [human-caused] global warming (AGW) hypothesis. Today, I am skeptical no longer. Like conservative blogger D.R. Tucker, on this issue, I was ultimately "defeated by facts." Today, converging arguments have persuaded me that AGW is real and that we must take action to prevent it.

Reading the 2007 Fourth Assessment Report of the Intergovernmental Panel on Climate Change [IPCC] was the critical moment in D.R. Tucker's conversion process. In my own case, I finally reached a point where I could no longer in good conscience deny the implications of the cumulative weight of so large a body of evidence.

That body of evidence is extensive, and growing. For example, in 2010 the National Academy of Sciences issued what has been dubbed "'the most comprehensive report ever on climate change.'" The National Academy of Sciences report echos many of the same findings as the earlier 2007 IPCC report but "reflect[s] a greater urgency because committee members had an additional five years of research to draw on." And in 2010, for the first time, the Pentagon identified AGW as a threat to our nation's security in its Quadrennial Defense Review. Indeed, just a few days ago [in May 2011], Australia's Climate Commission issued a new report examining recent scientific research and concluding that it is "critical" to reduce carbon emissions over the next decade as the economic and ecological impacts of AGW are already beginning to become evident.

Today, there is no debate in the scientific community about whether the Earth is warming—it is. There is also a nearly unanimous consensus that human activity is responsible for this warming.

Another critical element in my own conversion was the leading role being played by Pope Benedict XVI and the Catholic Church in articulating the moral imperative to address the threat posed by AGW. Earlier this month, a working group at the Pontifical Academy of Sciences issued a declaration calling on all people of good will "to recognize the serious and potentially irreversible impacts of global warming caused by the anthropogenic emissions of greenhouse gases and other pollutants, and by changes in forests, wetlands, grasslands, and other land uses." And the Pope himself highlighted the "problems associated with climate change" and the need for collective action to address them in his January, 2010 World Day of Peace message. Taken as a whole, Catholic thought and teaching on the environment illuminated for me the fact that caring for the natural world, and an ethic of responsible stewardship towards it, were integral components of an authentically pro-life worldview.

In the end, my own extensive reading and research on AGW made the following conclusions inescapable: today, there is no debate in the scientific community about whether the Earth is warming—it is. There is also a nearly unanimous consensus that human activity is responsible for this warming. There is some debate, at the margins, over the severity of the consequences that will inure from this and whether we can take any remedial measures that will slow, stop, or reverse this process. The consensus position, however, is clear—AGW will probably have a significant negative impact on human civilization and the natural world, and there are practical steps that could be taken now to avoid this fate. Given the foregoing, addressing AGW today is an ethical and moral imperative. Failing to do so is a repudiation of our responsibilities both to each other, to the poor, and most particularly, to future generations. It is a breach of faith, trust, and duty, of enormous magnitude.

The Role of Ideology

Regrettably, while the scientific evidence supporting AGW has become increasingly more persuasive over the past several years, and the need for immediate action ever more apparent, public opinion, at least in the United States, has been trending in the opposite direction.

A sustained movement by conservatives willing to speak out on climate issues . . . is critical to breaking through the ideological prism through which many conservatives view [anthropogenic global warming] today.

I think there are several reasons for this. First, few of us (myself included) possess the technical expertise or knowledge required to independently assess and analyze scientific research, reports, or peer reviewed literature. As a result, we fall back on pop-culture works, like the thoroughly debunked book "Cool It," and reports in the mainstream media. The climate denial industry has exploited this by endeavoring to create "doubt" in the minds of Americans, despite the fact that no reasonable grounds for doubt remain. Meanwhile, the scientific community has not been particularly effective at communicating the case for AGW in a way that is accessible and understandable to most Americans. At the same time, the radicalization of the political Right, and the rise to prominence of an extreme form of libertarianism within its ranks, has made opposition to AGW a required [tenet] of its political orthodoxy. In other words, our political ideology demands that it cannot be true—therefore, it is not.

The rejection of proven science in favor of a form of ideologically driven magical thinking by the GOP [Republican Party] is extremely unfortunate, and unnecessary. As D.R. Tucker has observed, "It does not put America on the road to serfdom to suggest that the federal government has a compelling interest in protecting the country from ecological damage. If anything, it puts America on the road to common sense." Similarly, the embrace of climate denialism by the GOP today represents a rejection of the traditional conservative concern for preserving and extending the stability of communities and institutions over time—of stewardship for society. As David Jenkins has pointedly noted: "The policies being peddled by these folks reflect a live for today–let me do what I want mentality that has nothing to do with the conservative notion of protecting the interests of future generations."

Given the foregoing, there is a moral imperative of the most urgent nature for all people of good will, and particularly Republicans, to speak out on AGW and the threats that it poses. Collectively, we must work to better inform the public and expose them to the scientific research on this issue. In this regard, we should keep in mind Edward Tufte's use of the [1986 space shuttle] *Challenger* disaster as a case study in the importance of organizing and communicating complex information effectively. Here, that means making the case for AGW in a way that is both powerful and persuasive to the average person. In addition, part of the effort must be a sustained movement by conservatives willing to speak out on climate issues—this is critical to breaking through the ideological prism through which many conservatives view AGW today. Another element of this effort is networking—there is no reason for any conservative climate change convert to feel alone! Thankfully, there is an organization for Republicans concerned about AGW, and the anti-science agenda being pursued by loud segments within the GOP—Republicans for Environmental Protection—and I am proud to serve as its Coordinator here in Delaware.

I want to close with a cautionary tale that has deeply informed my own thinking on AGW and environmental policy—one based on the profound implications of remarks made by Dr. Paul Crutzen in his 1995 Nobel Prize lecture. Dr. Crutzen earned his Nobel Prize for his research on the damage caused to the Earth's ozone layer by CFCs [chlorofluorocarbons]. Dr. Crutzen's lecture includes information on the role of chance in determining the extent of human impacts on complex natural systems—one that should cause climate-deniers to pause, and reflect. In his lecture, Dr. Crutzen noted that, had the chemical industry simply developed "organobromide compounds rather than CFCs" then "without any preparedness" humanity would have been faced with the destruction of most of the ozone layer before the scientific community had the ability to analyze and measure the problem. Obviously, this would have had a catastrophic impact on life on Earth. Reflecting on the [role] of pure chance in avoiding this outcome, Dr. Crutzen "conclude[d] that mankind has been extremely lucky." For me, Dr. Crutzen's remarks highlight the need for prudence and responsible stewardship in environmental policy, and with respect to AGW.

I am a climate change convert, and I know I'm not alone. Today, we must work with renewed vigor to better educate the public on the threat posed by AGW, and to build support for policies designed to eliminate or mitigate it. However, given the scope of threat posed by AGW, time is not our ally. We need to hurry. There's no telling how much longer our luck will hold.

CHAPTER 3

What Are the Predicted Impacts of Global Warming?

Chapter Preface

Climate scientists have predicted that extreme weather events—such as heat waves, drought, floods, and intense storms, hurricanes, and tornadoes—will become the hallmark of climate changes that global warming will bring in coming years. In 2011, the United States broke records for extreme weather, and many people wondered whether these events were the first sign of climate-change impacts in this country.

The United States National Oceanic and Atmospheric Administration (NOAA), the nation's main weather agency, announced in January 2012 that the United States experienced a record fourteen major weather and climate disasters in 2011—each of which caused more than $1 billion in damages, as well as the loss of human life and property. This surpasses the 2008 record of nine disasters costing at least $1 billion. The weather events in 2011 included a blizzard, killer tornadoes, historic heat waves and drought, wildfires, and floods. Altogether, extreme weather in 2011 cost approximately $53 billion in damages and resulted in eight thousand injuries and more than one thousand deaths.

The year 2011 began with the Groundhog Day blizzard, a powerful winter storm that hit the central, eastern, and northeastern states from January 29 through February 3. The storm brought blizzard conditions and more than two feet of snow to the city of Chicago and circulated cold air and heavy snowfall across a large swath of the country—from New Mexico and Texas to the Midwest and New England states. An ice storm preceded a warm front that contained most of the snow, making road and flight conditions especially treacherous and knocking down power lines and collapsing roofs. Many power outages were reported along with flight cancellations and school and business closures. Insured losses from the storm exceeded $1 billion, but total losses were estimated at $1.8 billion. In addition, 36 deaths were attributed to the storm, many of them from shoveling snow or auto accidents.

The spring of 2011 saw a string of dangerous tornadoes rip through the Midwest and Southeast. Altogether, there were 1,897 tornadoes reported in the country in 2011—the most ever recorded—and 7 extremely large tornadoes were especially destructive. The first of these occurred on April 4–5, when 46 tornadoes swept across the nation's midsection, causing 9 deaths and insured losses of $2 billion, and a total of $2.8 billion in damages. A few days later, from April 8 to 11, 59 tornadoes were reported in central and southern states. This outbreak caused insured losses of more than $1.5 billion and total losses of more than $2.2 billion but fortunately no fatalities. A third set of tornadoes from April 14 to 16, again in central and southern states, caused 38 deaths and another $1.4 billion in insured losses and more than $2.1 billion in total losses. The month of April closed with yet another tornado outbreak in the central and southern states, April 25–28, with 343 tornadoes reported, which resulted in 321 deaths, 240 of which occurred in Alabama alone. This outbreak caused more than $7.3 billion in insured losses and total losses of more than $10.2 billion.

The month of May brought yet another group of 180 tornadoes in the central and southern states on May 22–27. This time, Joplin, Missouri, took the brunt of the damage—suffering 158 fatalities, the deadliest single tornado event recorded in the United States since modern record-keeping began in 1950. All together, the May tornadoes cost more than $6.5 billion in insured losses, and more than $9.1 billion in total losses. The tornado season continued with a set of 81 tornadoes that hit the central United States on June 18–22, killing three people and causing more than $1 billion in insured losses, and more than $1.3 billion in total damages. More severe storms hit the areas east of the Rocky Mountains beginning on July 10, bringing a final outbreak of tornadoes, hail, high winds across the central states of Colorado, Wyoming, Iowa, Illinois, Missouri, Minnesota, and Ohio. Losses totaled more than $1 billion and two people died.

Some of the same storms that spawned the 2011 tornadoes also caused above-average precipitation that combined with melting snow to cause devastating floods along the Mississippi River and its tributaries. In April and May 2011, these storms dumped record levels of rainfall, causing the Mississippi and other rivers and streams to rise in a number of states, including Illinois, Missouri, Kentucky, Tennessee, Arkansas, Mississippi, and Louisiana. Parts of Kentucky, Tennessee, and Mississippi were declared federal disaster areas, and a large spillway in Louisiana was intentionally flooded in order to save the cities of Baton Rouge and New Orleans. Tens of thousands of homes were placed under evacuation orders, and hundreds of people were killed in the storms. Later, the summer storm that hit the central part of the country caused similar flooding along the Missouri and Souris Rivers, damaging thousands of acres of farmland, flooding thousands of homes, and causing an estimated eleven thousand people to evacuate in North Dakota. Losses from this flooding exceeded $1 billion and caused at least 5 deaths.

While the midwestern, central, and southeastern parts of the United States grappled with intense storms, tornadoes, and flooding, the Southwest experienced hot temperatures and a severe drought. The dry conditions were attributed to a strong La Niña—a periodic climatic phenomenon created by cooling in the tropical Pacific Ocean that affects weather around the world. States such as Texas, Oklahoma, New Mexico, Arizona, southern Kansas, and western Louisiana were hit the hardest. The drought dried up wells, pastures, and farmland, causing close to $10 billion in direct losses of crops, livestock, and timber. The drought was so intense that some commentators compared it with the Dust Bowl, a severe drought that hit the Great Plains region in the 1930s. In addition, the heat and drought created conditions that resulted in historic wildfires in Texas, New Mexico, and Arizona. Three destructive mega-fires in these states burned millions of acres, causing 5 deaths and losses of more than $1 billion.

Mother Nature had even more in store for the United States in 2011, however. In August, Hurricane Irene, a Category 1 hurricane (downgraded from a Category 3), hit the coast of North Carolina and then moved north along the Atlantic coast to Virginia, Maryland, and New York City, bringing with it high winds, torrential rainfall, and floods. The storm knocked out power to more than 7 million homes, caused more than $7.3 billion in damages, and killed forty-five people. A smaller but still deadly storm, Tropical Storm Lee, in September 2011 caused wind and flood damage in both the Southeast and the Northeast, causing total losses of more than $1 billion and 21 deaths.

Climate scientists say that extreme weather is consistent with what global warming might bring, but they are reluctant to blame individual weather events on global climate change. The authors of the viewpoints included in the following chapter discuss extreme weather and describe some of the other impacts of global warming that may already be happening, as well as impacts that are expected in the future.

Many Climate Impacts Predicted by the IPCC Are Already Happening

National Aeronautics and Space Administration

The National Aeronautics and Space Administration (NASA) is the US government agency that runs the civilian arm of the nation's space program. As part of its mission, it conducts research on global warming.

Global climate change has already had observable effects on the environment. Glaciers have shrunk, ice on rivers and lakes is breaking up earlier, plant and animal ranges have shifted and trees are flowering sooner.

Effects that scientists had predicted in the past would result from global climate change are now occuring: loss of sea ice, accelerated sea level rise and longer, more intense heat waves.

Scientists have high confidence that global temperatures will continue to rise for decades to come, largely due to greenhouse gasses produced by human activities. The Intergovernmental Panel on Climate Change (IPCC), which includes more than 1,300 scientists from the United States and other countries, forecasts a temperature rise of 2.5 to 10 degrees Fahrenheit over the next century.

According to the IPCC, the extent of climate change effects on individual regions will vary over time and with the ability of different societal and environmental systems to mitigate or adapt to change.

The IPCC predicts that increases in global mean temperature of less than 1.8 to 5.4 degrees Fahrenheit (1 to 3 degrees Celsius) above 1990 levels will produce beneficial impacts in some regions and harmful ones in others. Net annual costs will increase over time as global temperatures increase.

By 2020, between 75 and 250 million people are projected to be exposed to increased water stress [in Africa.]

"Taken as a whole," the IPCC states, "the range of published evidence indicates that the net damage costs of climate change are likely to be significant and to increase over time."

Below are some of the regional impacts of global change forecast by the IPCC:

- *North America*: Decreasing snowpack in the western mountains; 5–20 percent increase in yields of rain-fed agriculture in some regions; increased frequency, intensity and duration of heat waves in cities that currently experience them.

- *Latin America*: Gradual replacement of tropical forest by savannah in eastern Amazonia; risk of significant biodiversity loss through species extinction in many tropical areas; significant changes in water availability for human consumption, agriculture and energy generation.

- *Europe*: Increased risk of inland flash floods; more frequent coastal flooding and increased erosion from storms and sea level rise; glacial retreat in mountainous areas; reduced snow cover and winter tourism; extensive species losses; reductions of crop productivity in southern Europe.

- *Africa*: By 2020, between 75 and 250 million people are projected to be exposed to increased water stress; yields from rain-fed agriculture could be reduced by up to 50 percent in some regions by 2020; agricultural production, including access to food, may be severely compromised.

- *Asia*: Freshwater availability projected to decrease in Central, South, East and Southeast Asia by the 2050s; coastal areas will be at risk due to increased flooding; death rate from disease associated with floods and droughts expected to rise in some regions.

Global Climate Change: Recent Impacts

Phenomena	*Likelihood that trend occurred in late 20th century*
• Cold days, cold nights and frost less frequent over land areas	Very likely
• More frequent hot days and nights	Very likely
• Heat waves more frequent over most land areas	Likely
• Increased incidence of extreme high sea level	Likely
• Global area affected by drought has increased (since 1970s)	Likely in some regions
• Increase in intense tropical cyclone activity in North Atlantic (since 1970)	Likely in some regions

Global Climate Change: Future Trends

Phenomena	*Likelihood of trend*
• Contraction of snow cover areas, increased thaw in permafrost regions, decrease in sea ice extent	Virtually certain
• Increased frequency of hot extremes, heat waves and heavy precipitation	Very likely to occur
• Increase in tropical cyclone intensity	Likely to occur
• Precipitation increases in high latitudes	Very likely to occur

Phenomena	*Likelihood of trend*
• Precipitation decreases in sub-tropical land regions	Very likely to occur
• Decreased water resources in many semi-arid areas, including western U.S. and Mediterranean basin	High confidence

Definitions of likelihood ranges used to express the assessed probability of occurrence: *virtually certain* >99%, *very likely* >90%, *likely* >66%.

Snow and Ice Are Decreasing in the Northern Hemisphere at Twice the Rate Predicted by Climate Models

Pete Spotts

Pete Spotts is a staff writer for the Christian Science Monitor, *a daily US newspaper published by the Christian Science Publishing Society.*

A long-term retreat in snow and ice cover in the Northern Hemisphere is weakening the ability of these seasonal cloaks of white to reflect sunlight back into space and cool global climate, according to a study published this week [January 15, 2011].

Indeed, over the past 30 years, the cooling effect from this so-called cryosphere—essentially areas covered by snow and ice at least part of the year—appears to have weakened at more than twice the pace projected by global climate models, the research team conducting the work estimates.

The study, which appeared online Sunday in the journal *Nature Geoscience*, represents a first cut at trying to calculate from direct measurements the impact of climate change on the Northern Hemisphere's cryosphere. The study was conducted by a team of federal and university scientists who examined data gathered between 1979 and 2008.

Of particular interest is a self-reinforcing process, or feedback, through which warming reduces snow and ice cover. Those reductions expose more ocean and landscape to sunlight during spring, summer and fall. After absorbing the sunlight, these exposed features radiate the heat back into the atmosphere. This accelerates the loss of snow and ice already triggered by global warming.

Because the Arctic is warmer than its southern counterpart, small changes in temperatures at the top of the world have a relatively larger effect on ice and snow cover.

Pinning down the size of this effect—one of three major feedbacks in the global climate process—is important in understanding how much the global climate could warm in response to rising concentrations of greenhouse gases that human activities have pumped into the atmosphere, explains Mark Serreze director of the National Snow and Ice Data Center in Boulder, Colo.

Over the past decade or more, other teams have tracked the decline of snow and ice cover in the Northern Hemisphere, the northward march at high latitudes of vegetation typically found farther south, and other changes that suggest the feedback has kicked in.

This latest study says "yes, the feedback is working as we suspected it would be," says Dr. Serreze, who was not part of the team conducting the research. "But it also argues that maybe the feedback is stronger than we thought it would be."

That last point will likely be challenged, he adds, as part of the scientific process.

"Putting numbers to these feedbacks is a tough thing to do," he says. Still, "this is an important paper. I see this as a significant advance in climate science."

As one of the world's two deep-freeze thermostats, Antarctica is still chiller-in-chief. But because the Arctic is warmer than its southern counterpart, small changes in temperatures at the top of the world have a relatively larger effect on ice and snow cover, researchers say.

Mark Flanner, a climate researcher at the University of Michigan who led the team, says the goal of the new study was to provide a reality check on global climate models' representations of the impact that declining snow and ice has on the Earth's so-called radiation budget. The radiation budget is a kind of bookkeeping process that tries to account for all the sunlight Earth receives and either reflects or converts into heat.

Using satellite measurements as well as field measurements of the extent of snow and ice cover, the team teased out details of seasonal patterns in the amount of solar radiation the Northern Hemisphere's snow and ice reflect.

The Albedo Problem

Snow appears to have its maximum cooling effect—reflecting the most sunlight back into space—in late spring, as the light strengthens but snow cover is still near its maximum extent for the year. Sea ice in the Arctic Ocean has its biggest effect in June, before its annual summer melt-back accelerates, explains Don Perovich, a researcher at the US Army Corps of Engineers Cold Regions Research and Engineering Laboratory in Hanover, N.H., and a member of the team reporting the results.

That means "it becomes important when you melt snow and ice," he says. "If you start that melting earlier, you tend to have a lower albedo every day throughout the summer," he says. Albedo is a measure of a surface's ability to reflect light.

Research published by a different team in 2009 showed that at least for the Canadian Archipelago, the melt season grew at a rate of about seven days per decade during the 1979–2008 period. Most of that expansion has come at season's end, the team reported, but the onset of the melt season was coming earlier as well.

But the eyebrow-arching moment for Dr. Flanner and his colleagues came in comparing real-world measurements of the ice-snow feedback with those from models.

Twice the Decline in Cooling Effect

According to the team, the measured decline in the cooling effect of the Northern Hemisphere's shrinking cryosphere associated with a 1-degree Celsius increase in Northern Hemisphere temperatures was more than twice that predicted by climate models.

"The reduction was somewhat surprising," Flanner says.

The team acknowledges that the study has its limitations.

For instance, the 30-year period "is right on the edge of being long enough" to separate long-term trends from year-to-year changes in conditions that occur naturally, Flanner says.

But Dr. Perovich adds that many of the assumptions the team had to make as it analyzed the data are likely to prove conservative.

US Farmers Dodge the Impacts of Global Warming—at Least for Now, Stanford Researcher Says

Louis Bergeron

Louis Bergeron is a staff member of the Stanford News Service, part of Stanford University's Office of University Communications, which handles media relations and disseminates the university's news.

Global warming is likely already taking a toll on world wheat and corn production, according to a new study led by Stanford University researchers. But the United States, Canada and northern Mexico have largely escaped the trend.

"It appears as if farmers in North America got a pass on the first round of global warming," said David Lobell, an assistant professor of environmental Earth system science at Stanford University. "That was surprising, given how fast we see weather has been changing in agricultural areas around the world as a whole."

Lobell and his colleagues examined temperature and precipitation records since 1980 for major crop-growing countries in the places and times of year when crops are grown. They then used crop models to estimate what worldwide crop yields would have been had temperature and precipitation had typical fluctuations around 1980 levels.

The researchers found that global wheat production was 5.5 percent lower than it would have been had the climate remained stable, and global corn production was lower by almost 4 percent. Global rice and soybean production were not significantly affected.

The United States, which is the world's largest producer of soybeans and corn, accounting for roughly 40 percent of global production, experienced a very slight cooling trend and no significant production impacts.

Total worldwide relative losses of [wheat and corn] equal the annual production of corn in Mexico and wheat in France.

Outside of North America, most major producing countries were found to have experienced some decline in wheat and corn (or maize) yields related to the rise in global temperature. "Yields in most countries are still going up, but not as fast as we estimate they would be without climate trends," Lobell said.

Lobell is the lead author of a paper about the research published May 5 online in *Science Express*.

Russia, India and France suffered the greatest drops in wheat production relative to what might have been with no global warming. The largest comparative losses in corn production were seen in China and Brazil.

Total worldwide relative losses of the two crops equal the annual production of corn in Mexico and wheat in France. Together, the four crops in the study—wheat, corn, soybeans and rice—constitute approximately 75 percent of the calories that humans worldwide consume, directly or indirectly through livestock, according to research cited in the study.

"Given the relatively small temperature trends in the U.S. Corn Belt, it shouldn't be surprising if complacency or even skepticism about global warming has set in, but this study suggests that would be misguided," Lobell said.

Since 1950, the average global temperature has increased at a rate of roughly 0.13 degrees Celsius per decade. But over the next two to three decades average global temperature is expected to rise approximately 50 percent faster than that, according to the report of the Intergovernmental Panel on Climate Change. With that rate of temperature change, it is unlikely that the crop-growing regions of the United States will continue to escape the rising temperatures, Lobell said.

"The climate science is still unclear about why summers in the Corn Belt haven't been warming. But most explanations suggest that warming in the future is just as likely there as elsewhere in the world," Lobell said.

"In other words, farmers in the Corn Belt seem to have been lucky so far."

The effects of climate change on crop yields have caused an increase of approximately 20 percent in global market prices.

This is the first study to come up with a global estimate for the past 30 years of what has been happening, Lobell said.

To develop their estimates, the researchers used publicly available global data sets from the United Nations Food and Agriculture Organization and from the University of Delaware, University of Wisconsin, and McGill University.

The researchers also estimated the economic effects of the changes in crop yield using models of commodity markets.

"We found that since 1980, the effects of climate change on crop yields have caused an increase of approximately 20 percent in global market prices," said Wolfram Schlenker, an economist at Columbia University and a coauthor of the paper in *Science*.

He said if the beneficial effects of higher carbon dioxide levels on crop growth are factored into the calculation, the increase drops down to 5 percent.

"Five percent sounds small until you realize that at current prices world production of these four crops are together worth nearly $1 trillion per year," Schlenker said. "So a price increase of 5 percent implies roughly $50 billion per year more spent on food."

Rising commodity prices have so far benefited American farmers, Lobell and Schlenker said, because they haven't suffered the relative declines in crop yield that the rest of the world has been experiencing.

"It will be interesting to see what happens over the next decade in North America," Lobell said. "But to me the key message is not necessarily the specifics of each country. I think the real take-home message is that climate change is not just about the future, but that it is affecting agriculture now. Accordingly, efforts to adapt agriculture such as by developing more heat- and drought-tolerant crops will have big payoffs, even today."

Justin Costa-Roberts, an undergraduate student at Stanford, is also a coauthor of the *Science* paper. David Lobell is a researcher in Stanford's Program on Food Security and the Environment, a joint program of Stanford's Woods Institute for the Environment and Freeman Spogli Institute for International Studies. Schlenker is an assistant professor at the School of International and Public Affairs and at the Department of Economics at Columbia.

The work was supported by a grant from the Rockefeller Foundation.

Global Warming Is Increasing World Food Prices

Damian Carrington

Damian Carrington is a reporter and the head of environment at the Guardian, *a daily newspaper out of Manchester, England.*

Global warming has already harmed the world's food production and has driven up food prices by as much as 20% over recent decades, new research has revealed.

The drop in the productivity of crop plants around the world was not caused by changes in rainfall but was because higher temperatures can cause dehydration, prevent pollination and lead to slowed photosynthesis.

Lester Brown, president of the Earth Policy Institute, Washington DC, said the findings indicate a turning point: "Agriculture as it exists today evolved over 11,000 years of reasonably stable climate, but that climate system is no more." Adaptation is difficult because our knowledge of the future is not strong enough to drive new investments, he said, "so we just keep going, hoping for the best."

The scientists say their work shows how crucial it is to find ways to adapt farming to a warmer world, to ensure that rises in global population are matched by rising food production. "It is vital," said Wolfram Schlenker, [a professor] at Columbia University in New York and one of the research team. "If we continue to have the same seed varieties and temperatures continue to rise, then food prices will rise further. [Addressing] that is the big question."

The new research joins a small number of studies in which the fingerprint of climate change has been separated from natural variations in weather and other factors, demonstrating that the effects of warming have already been felt in the world. Scientists have shown that the chance of the severe heatwave that killed thousands in Europe in 2003 was made twice as likely by global warming, while other work showed that the floods that caused £3.5bn [3.5 billion pounds Sterling, or about $5.5 billion] of damage in England in 2000 were made two to three times more likely.

Rising temperatures affected the annual crop yields of all major producer nations between 1980 and 2008.

Food prices have reached new record highs this year, and have been implicated as a trigger for unrest in the Middle East and Africa. A rising appetite for meat is a critical factor, said Schlenker. "We actually have enough calories to feed the world quite comfortably, the problem is meat is really inefficient," as many kilogrammes of grain are needed to produce one kilogramme of meat, he said. "As countries get richer and have a preference for meat, which is more expensive, they price people in poorer countries out of the market."

"The research provides evidence of big shifts in wheat and maize production," commented Prof Tim Wheeler at the Walker Institute for Climate System Research, Reading University, UK [United Kingdom], who added it had involved "heroic" statistical analysis. But he said that, while long-term climate change impacts were another pressure on food prices, short-term price spikes were linked to extreme weather events, such as the Russian heatwaves and wildfires in 2010.

The study, published in the journal *Science*, examined how rising temperatures affected the annual crop yields of all major producer nations between 1980 and 2008. Computer models were used to show how much grain would have been harvested in the absence of warming. Overall, yields have been rising over the last decades and the models took this into account. The scientists found that global wheat production was 33m tonnes [metric tons] (5.5%) lower than it would have been without warming and maize production was 23m tonnes (3.8%) lower. Specific countries fared worse than the average, with Russia losing 15% of its potential wheat crop, and Brazil, Mexico and Italy suffering above average losses. Some countries experienced lower production of rice and soybeans, although these drops were offset by gains in other countries.

The losses drove up food prices by as much as 18.9%, the team calculated, although the rise could be as low as 6.4% if the increased carbon dioxide in the atmosphere strongly boosts plant growth and yields—a factor that is not well understood by scientists.

Global food prices have risen by about 200% in recent years, says Schlenker. Other causes of the rise are the increased demand for meat and the diversion of food into biofuels. Nonetheless, the researchers conclude that the negative impact on crops overall is "likely to be incurring large economic and health costs".

US Production Not Affected

The US, which has the world's largest share of overall production, stood out in the analysis because it appears to have lost no production to climate change as yet. Schlenker said this was because the rise in temperature there was very small compared to other parts of the world. This was perhaps due simply to luck with the weather, or the cooling influence of aerosol particles, such as soot, that blocks warming.

"US farmers are having a good time in the sense that their yields have not been impacted much and prices have been pretty high, so for them it has been pretty profitable," he said. "But most climate models predict that eventually the US will warm."

Adapting farming to climate change could involve moving to cooler areas as existing areas warm, said Schlenker, but often soils are poorer in the new locations. He highlighted the potential of biotechnology—genetic engineering—to develop new crop varieties that are more resistant to heat, but said the potential remains unproven. "What happens over the next 20 years depends on how optimistic you are about finding those extra ways of adapting."

Global Warming Will Likely Cause Serious Human Health Effects

Thilaka Ravi

Thilaka Ravi is a reporter for MedIndia.net, an India-based website that provides essential health-related information to health-care consumers and medical professionals.

The world is spinning in a vicious cycle of demand and supply that is both the cause and effect of global warming. If the situation continues, health hazards will increase.

Global warming is all about adverse climate change caused by the trapping of greenhouse gases (like carbon dioxide) in the earth's atmosphere that affects biodiversity and poses a serious health hazard. Countermeasures to facilitate living in hotter temperatures like air-conditioning and refrigeration will unfortunately consume more electricity from power plants that burn coal, releasing carbon dioxide. This will further spike global warming and have a seriously damaging influence on human health.

Naturally occurring greenhouse gases such as carbon dioxide, water vapor, methane, ozone and nitrous oxide hold heat in the atmosphere creating a greenhouse effect and keep the earth warm enough to sustain life. Enhanced greenhouse effect or the abnormal increase of 'greenhouse gases' due to human activities like burning of solid waste; wood; fossil fuels like oil, natural gas and coal; deforestation and the release of hydrofluorocarbons (HFCs), perfluorocarbons (PFCs), and sulfur hexafluoride (SF_6) from industrial processes cause more than normal heat to be trapped in the atmosphere and cause global warming.

Effects of Global Warming

Climatic changes triggered by global warming can bring in their wake extreme conditions like abnormal storms, drought and floods and can be of immediate threat to life [and health.]

If the globe continues to sizzle unchecked, extreme weather conditions will cause infectious diseases and death worldwide.

Recent outbreaks of malaria, dengue fever ("breakbone" fever), Hanta virus and similar diseases in the West due to climate change are the consequences of global warming, according to some Harvard Medical School doctors. The incidence of kidney stones is likely to go up and so are many other conditions. The long-term serious consequence to human health is likely to threaten our very existence on this planet. Read some of the alarming facts related to it:

- Extreme temperatures caused by climate change can directly cause death, as in heat strokes—especially in the old and the young. Studies based on earlier heat wave events predict a 145% increase in deaths in New York.

- Adverse impact of climate stress on agriculture worldwide may add 300 million victims of malnutrition to the existing number.

- Intergovernmental Panel on Climate Change (IPCC) scientists project that warmer climates will increase malaria-carrying mosquitoes and put 65% of the world's population at risk of malarial infection—an increase of 20% from the 1990s.

- Warm temperatures will aggravate air and water pollution and pose health hazards.

- Some researchers predict algal blooms could occur more often—especially in polluted sea waters—and cause infectious diseases like cholera.

In brief, global warming can soon become a risk factor for heat strokes, cardiovascular and respiratory problems. People with an ailing heart are especially vulnerable because the cardiovascular system has to work harder to cool the body in very hot weather. A heat wave in July 1995 killed more than 700 people in the Chicago area alone.

High air temperatures increase the ozone concentration at ground level. The natural ozone layer in the upper atmosphere protects the earth from the sun's harmful ultraviolet radiation; but at ground level ozone becomes a harmful pollutant that damages lung tissue and aggravates asthma and other breathing diseases. Even in healthy individuals exposure to modest levels of ozone can cause nausea, chest pain and pulmonary congestion.

One school of scientists warn that if the globe continues to sizzle unchecked, extreme weather conditions will cause infectious diseases and death worldwide. However, there is another school of health experts who believe that global warming is a convenient scapegoat for putting the blame on increasing incidence of infectious diseases. They list other factors that are contributing to this increase that include:

- Increasing disregard for public health practices (even simple things like washing hands)

- Overcrowding of cities

- Rise in population of vectors such as mosquitoes and ticks—due to inadequate control measures

- Increased international travel by people that can take viruses across the hemisphere

- Genetic mutation in bacteria and viruses

Developed nations have the ability and infrastructure to quickly identify and take adequate measures to curb the problems that can result from global warming. Examples include emergency measures such as moving people suffering from heat-stroke to air-conditioned rooms and stringent action to reduce the emission of photochemical compounds that cause ground-level ozone. Developing and underdeveloped countries are seriously handicapped in these areas of infrastructure and failure to draft and implement stringent laws against factories for adding to pollution and global warming.

What Can Be Done as "Global Citizens"

As global citizens of this beautiful planet we need to take immediate steps to control global temperatures from reaching dangerously high levels. We can do our own bit by helping out, and some of the measures include:

- Using less fossil fuels and electricity—switch off lights, fans, air-conditioners, computers etc. when not required

- Buying energy-efficient products such as compact fluorescent light (CFL) bulbs

- Recycling paper, plastics and whatever we can

- Planting more trees

- Using solar heaters to heat water

- Harnessing alternate sources of "clean" energy—such as solar and wind energy—that do not emit carbon dioxide are some sure ways to reduce global warming

- Avoid wastage of food and water.

Global Warming Poses a Grave Threat to Wildlife

E. Jean Brennan

E. Jean Brennan is a climate change scientist with Defenders of Wildlife, a wildlife conservation organization that works to save wildlife and to defend the Endangered Species Act.

Human-induced global warming is emerging as the greatest threat facing the planet today. Wildlife is especially vulnerable. Negative impacts of climate change are already evident, including loss of critical habitat in the polar and high mountain ecosystems; damage to oceans, coastlines and coral reefs due to sea level rise and increased storm activity; and more frequent and intense periods or drought. . . .

The challenges associated with climate change due to global warming are negatively affecting both the physical and biological elements of nature. The impacts of sea-level rise associated with climate change alone present not only an ecological challenge, but also a social, economic and cultural threat exceeding anything mankind has ever faced. . . .

The Earth's climate system is extremely responsive to changes in temperature. As a result, global warming is affecting climate patterns and has already changed the physical world. For example, as a result of rising temperatures, lakes are freezing later, spring ice is breaking up earlier, glaciers are retreating and the Arctic ice cap is melting.

The polar region has seen the greatest rise in temperature and is already suffering the most extreme climate impacts. In recent years, the Arctic has experienced a dramatic decline of sea ice, especially during summer. The increased flow of fresh water into the oceans via surface runoff from melting snow and ice has caused sea levels to rise globally, although at different rates geographically. The greatest rise is on the Atlantic and Gulf coasts of North America. Rising sea levels and increasing storm and wave intensity are claiming coastal and salt marsh habitats. Salt marsh habitats along shorelines in the temperate zone are increasingly inundated. As a result, the ability of many areas to function and sustain critical ecosystem services is compromised.

Other changes in the physical world not directly attributed to global warming, but correlated with temperature increases and decreased precipitation, are the increased incidence and intensity of storms and wildfires. In the western United States, for example, the incidence and intensity of wildfires are increasing following longer, hotter and drier summers and earlier snowmelt. The frequency and intensity of hurricanes are also showing strong correlation to increased land and sea surface temperatures.

As warming continues, . . . ranges of boreal species and resources are likely to be either significantly reduced in abundance or eliminated altogether.

Arctic and Boreal Impacts

Alaska clearly represents "ground zero" for global warming in North America, according to Glenn Juday of the University of Alaska and Deborah Williams of Alaska Conservation Solutions. Loss of sea ice is particularly evident, threatening the polar bear (*Ursus maritimus*) and other ice-dependent species. Ice-dependent species lose both the quality and quantity of physical sea-ice habitat. They can also lose access to their prey. For example, polar bears rely on the ice platform to hunt ringed and bearded seals (*Phocidae*). Seals frequent the thin edges and openings in the ice—breathing holes—where polar bears lie in wait. Now, however, due to the rise in surface and sea temperatures, less ice is forming, making it more difficult for bears to hunt and requiring them to expend more energy to swim between widely separated ice packs in search of prey. It is also increasingly difficult for female polar bears to acquire food and to successfully reproduce and rear their young.

Loss of sea ice also affects prey species. For seals, sea ice interacts with oceanography to enhance prey production in cold marine environments. As sea ice declines, so do the numbers within fish populations that sustain these seal populations. Seals either move farther out to sea or decline in numbers. These impacts of global warming are causing a cascading collapse of this Arctic system.

Terrestrial ecosystems in the Arctic are also showing impacts from global warming. Alaska is a world centerpiece for boreal species and genetic diversity. Climate changes evident in the state due to global warming are unprecedented in recent history. "The biggest change in the boreal region of the last several thousand years is underway now," said Glenn Juday. Tree growth on boreal forest sites is decreasing and, as temperatures continue to warm, is nearing absolute lethal limits. Fire and insect outbreaks have reached record-high levels with massive tree die-offs across thousands of acres. Because of warming, tundra is now flush with more combustible vegetation and tundra habitats are, in fact, burning.

By all indications, these changes to the boreal forest will not only continue but also intensify. As warming continues, biomes in much of boreal Alaska and northwest Canada are highly likely to shift within a decade. The ranges of boreal species and resources are likely to be either significantly reduced in abundance or eliminated altogether. Boreal forests are one system with potential to "flip"—to change completely in character and function. The western North American boreal region, for example, could change from a spruce/moose/beaver ecosystem to a grassland/bison/elk ecosystem. There is no known compensation mechanism to alter completely this trajectory of loss and change.

Marine and Coastal Impacts

In his global survey of climate impacts on marine and coastal ecosystems, Charles "Pete" Peterson of the University of North Carolina noted that global warming will negatively impact everything from the smallest plankton species that sustain the Arctic food web to the delicate, symbiotic algae that nourish tropical corals. It will also cause fundamental changes within the broader marine environment.

Plankton species have an upper temperature tolerance limit. As sea surface temperatures increase, the limits of their southern ranges in the Northern Hemisphere are moving progressively northward year after year. These changes in distribution are also evident in the fish and marine mammal species that feed on phytoplankton and zooplankton. Increased ocean temperatures are further threatening marine communities as novel conditions enhance the incidence and spread of disease.

Warm tropical ocean regions of the world are not immune to climate change impacts. If Alaska and the Arctic are "ground zero" in terrestrial ecosystems, then coral reefs are the "frontlines" of the global warming battle in the marine environment. This is evident most profoundly in what are widely known as coral reef "bleaching events." Bleaching occurs when the algae, which coexist within the coral and help to build its skeletal structure, move out of the coral as ocean temperatures rise above a threshold. The white coral skeleton remains, giving the reefs a bleached appearance due to the loss of the bright-hued algae that once colored it. If ocean temperatures remain high for too long, the algal colony does not return and the coral dies. Coral death can precipitate the collapse of the commensal marine community composed of myriad fish and marine invertebrates.

Bleaching events have now become an annual occurrence in many parts of the world. Current estimates in the Indo-

Pacific ocean region indicate a loss of more than half the coral cover in the last 30 to 40 years.

A most disturbing result of recent studies is the realization that increases in atmospheric carbon dioxide (CO_2) levels change the ocean chemistry and threaten the entire marine food chain. As part of the Earth's natural carbon balance, oceans absorb atmospheric CO_2. The excess CO_2 in the atmosphere is now being absorbed in the ocean, increasing pH levels, a process now referred to as "ocean acidification." These more acidic conditions reduce the availability of calcium carbonate, a critical compound many organisms at the base of the food chain need to build their cell coverings or outer skeletal structure. As a result of ocean acidification, entire marine invertebrate communities could literally dissolve.

A critical climatic factor in the tropics is not so much rising temperature, but rather loss of moisture.

Tom Lovejoy of The Heinz Center considered the response of terrestrial species to climate changes in both temperate and tropical ecosystems. It is not surprising that tropical mountain glaciers are melting, but what has surprised scientists is that climate change impacts are observed even in tropical forests.

A critical climatic factor in the tropics is not so much rising temperature, but rather loss of moisture. The Monteverde cloud forest in Costa Rica is perhaps the most well-documented site to report correlated negative climate impacts. It is also perhaps the first known location to record the extinction of a species, the golden toad (*Bufo periglenes*), as a possible result of climate change brought about by global warming. Another example is the decline of the quetzal (*Pharomachrus mocinno*), the ornate bird found only in the mountain highlands of Central America. Until recently, this area was only hospitable to quetzals. Now, with temperatures warming, toucans (*Ramphastidae*) are expanding their range upward to elevations where they threaten to out-compete the quetzal. Fire ants, insects previously not seen in these cooler mountain regions, have also moved higher, challenging the reproductive success of the quetzal with swarms that prey on nestlings.

Terry Root from Stanford University reviewed impacts in temperate regions. Numerous studies have documented various changes such as altered flowering phenology in plants and changes in the timing of breeding, nesting and migration for many animals. Such changes can have profound impacts on the population numbers and demographics of species that have evolved together over time. These biotic communities are now vulnerable to falling out of synchrony as species may respond differently to changed environmental cues.

For example, plants that time flowering, pollination and seed production events to climatic factors may now respond more quickly than the bird populations that rely on these plant resources to rear their offspring. Animals may respond more to day length or light intensity cues that are not being influenced by global warming. Animal migrations and breeding may thus fall out of synch with the plant resources required to feed and rear offspring.

Cases of wildlife populations in decline due to global warming are not isolated; they are occurring in areas around the world. Although the impacts are varied, changes in the timing of events or behavioral changes in response to climate changes are well-documented, and data are statistically robust.

Global Warming Could Create Security Challenges for the US Military

Keith Randall

Keith Randall is the associate director of news and information services in the Division of Marketing and Communications at Texas A&M University.

Changing global climate due to ongoing and projected warming have great potential to impact U.S. naval forces worldwide, according to a panel report issued today [March 10, 2011,] that includes a Texas A&M University researcher.

A warming climate presents national and homeland security challenges that will require the U.S. military to adopt a new way of doing business, according to the report *National Security Implications of Climate Change for U.S. Naval Forces.* The report, issued by the National Research Council and requested by the Chief of Naval Operations, paints an ominous picture of disputes over national boundaries and exclusive economic zones, strains on naval capabilities due to increasing disaster assistance demands, vulnerabilities of naval coastal facilities to sea level rise, greater demands on America's international maritime partnerships, and a shortfall in naval capabilities and personnel trained to operate in the Arctic, says Mahlon "Chuck" Kennicutt II, professor of oceanography who was a member of the committee that authored the report.

The committee included retired military leaders, policy experts from private sector "think tanks" and university researchers and scientists. The committee, which met nine times over more than 12 months, heard testimony from a large number of military, private sector and scientific experts. It was asked to examine climate change impacts on our world and how these might affect U.S. Naval forces' (including the Navy, Marine Corps and the Coast Guard) operations and capabilities.

Rising sea levels could have wide ranging detrimental impacts on naval facilities now and in the future.

"We were given a broad mandate to look at how climate change could affect naval forces," Kennicutt says. "The U.S. military needs to know what the world will look like 20–30 years from now if it is to make the preparations today to cope with tomorrow's realities."

The report describes a range of realistic scenarios about what could happen if climate change continues to unfold as most scientists believe it will over the next few decades. Kennicutt says the committee took the United Nations Intergovernmental Panel on Climate Change (IPCC) most likely future scenarios as a basis for its deliberations.

"It is an eye-opening report and presents a rather foreboding series of possible outcomes as our planet warms and reacts to past and continued greenhouse gas emissions," Kennicutt said.

"The report brings to the attention of U.S. naval leadership areas that need attention in future planning and that will prepare the Navy for a warmer world."

Kennicutt points out that if the polar icecaps in Greenland and Antarctica continue to melt, sea levels around the world will dramatically rise. Rising sea levels could have wide ranging detrimental impacts on naval facilities now and in the future, the report says.

"Arctic sea ice is melting much faster than predicted just a few years ago, so much so that there could be a summer, ice-free Arctic Ocean in a matter of years," he explains.

Year-Round Ocean Passage

In the Arctic, the Northwest Passage could become seasonally ice-free, allowing for routine transiting of ocean going vessels across the Arctic Ocean. This would reduce shipping time by as much as one-third from Europe to Asia alone.

"How this affects homeland security and what it means for terrorists or contraband smugglers that have ill will toward the U.S. is largely unknown," Kennicutt adds.

"It would open large areas of the Arctic Ocean that were previously inaccessible to fishing, tourism, oil and gas exploration and possible environmental disasters. Studies suggest that as much as 30 percent of the world's remaining oil and gas reserves are above the Arctic Circle, so it seems inevitable that exploration, exploitation and transport of oil and gas in the region will increase."

The United Nations "Law of the Sea" Treaty allows countries to expand their seaward national boundaries, creating friction between Arctic nations, he points out. The Arctic is seen by many as the epicenter for conflicts related to the "Law of Sea" as the Arctic Ocean is ringed by eight nations.

He adds that conflict over new national boundaries in the Arctic has already strained our relations with Canada, since much of Canada's territory is in the Arctic and their claims overlap with U.S. claims. The U.S. considers the Northwest Passage international waters, whereas Canada sees them as within its national boundaries.

"How this will affect U.S. national and homeland security is open to debate, but it is clear that an ice-free summer Arctic will dramatically change the politics and military strategies of the north for the foreseeable future," Kennicutt says.

The committee also looked at how droughts and other weather disasters play a role in the military's human assistance/disaster relief activities, such as the role the military played in recent tsunami and earthquake incidents (though not climate related). In recent years, there has been a growing demand on the U.S. military to serve a lead role in disaster relief.

"Especially dire are predicted impacts of famines and other natural disasters on Africa and the movement of refugees into Europe," he explains. "Predictions suggest that over the next few decades droughts will be more severe, and so will storms such as hurricanes and typhoons, and this could put a severe strain on the military as it tries to respond to increasingly frequent natural disasters worldwide.

"How the U.S. military responds to a changing world will be critical to how prepared we are as a nation for a future that might look quite different than today," he notes. "The report looks at some rather dire situations that could become a reality in just a few short years, and will the U.S. naval forces be ready to respond?"

CHAPTER 4

What Actions Should Be Taken to Address Global Warming?

Chapter Preface

The Kyoto Protocol, a 1997 international agreement designed to slow global warming, was set to expire at the end of 2012. The Kyoto treaty set binding targets for thirty-seven industrialized countries and the European community for reducing greenhouse gas emissions. The treaty has long been criticized for failing to significantly reduce such emissions, largely because some of the world's largest emitters (such as China and India) were not included in the treaty, and the United States, the world's second-largest emitter, failed to ratify it and thus does not abide by it. Nevertheless, since it is basically the only international effort to address global warming, many countries hoped that the treaty would be extended beyond 2012. In December 2011, negotiators from countries around the world met in Durban, South Africa, for climate talks to decide on the treaty's fate. The outcome of that meeting—a controversial agreement called the Durban Platform—will determine the path of climate actions for the next decade and beyond.

The gist of the Durban Platform is that the participating countries agreed to extend the Kyoto Treaty by a period of five to eight years but without setting any binding emissions-reduction targets. Instead, an Ad Hoc Working Group will work to develop a new climate treaty by 2015—a treaty that will come into force by 2020. Most notably, any new treaty, unlike the Kyoto Protocol, will legally require the world's two biggest emitters—China and the United States—to cut emissions. The extension of the Kyoto Protocol also allows the carbon markets and other mechanisms that are already in place to continue for countries that wish to use them on a voluntary basis. In addition, the Durban Platform establishes a Green Climate Fund, an Adaptation Committee, and other mechanisms to help developing countries cope with climate change. Industrialized countries agreed at earlier meetings to contribute $100 billion annually to these efforts. Other matters included in the agreement at Durban involved programs to prevent deforestation using monetary payments to developing nations, modifications to carbon markets to include projects to capture and store emissions from power plants, and the creation of a technical body to investigate the issue of agriculture's role in global warming.

The reaction to the Durban agreement was mixed. The negotiators themselves characterized it as "a breakthrough on the future of the international community's response to climate change, whilst recognizing the urgent need to raise their collective level of ambition to reduce greenhouse gas emissions to keep the average global temperature rise below two degrees Celsius."[1] Optimists agree that the Durban Platform is groundbreaking, noting that it represents the first time that all countries, including the United States and major developing countries like China and India, have agreed to binding emission limits. Before the Durban talks, many observers worried that negotiators would only be able to agree on voluntary efforts, so the platform is a success in that it creates a clear roadmap for legally binding emissions reductions.

Critics, however, point out that the Durban Platform does virtually nothing to actually reduce emissions in the short run and instead defers any such action for almost a decade, until 2020, when a new treaty is projected to take effect. Climate scientists warn that postponing action on global warming in this way may mean that it will be impossible to limit global warming to 2 degrees Celsius—the goal of the talks and the level that scientists consider to be a safe or manageable level. Another decade of high emissions, many scientists predict, will result in 3.5 degrees Celsius of warming by the end of the century. In addition, only the European Union and a handful of other countries have plans to continue reducing emissions after 2012. The United States, China, and other developing nations will not be restricted, because they were never bound by the Kyoto Protocol in the first place, and other countries who did ratify it, such as Japan, Russia, and Canada,have already dropped out of it and thus will not be making efforts to limit their emissions during the extension. And many observers remain pessimistic about whether governments will be able to meet emissions targets in future years—even if they are legally binding—given the expected economic and political obstacles in countries such as the United States. For example, a future US president pressured by oil interests or public opinion could easily ignore or reject the Durban Platform.

The next set of climate talks are scheduled for December 2012 in the Persian Gulf nation of Qatar. At that point, the Ad Hoc Committee created in Durban will begin negotiating the next climate treaty. The world will be watching to see whether the Durban road map will ultimately be successful in saving the world from global warming. In the meantime, the void created by the lack of international action has caused many commentators to explore other ways to address global warming. The authors in this chapter describe some of these alternative ideas.

Notes

1. United Nations Climate Change Conference 2011, "Durban Conference Delivers Breakthrough in International Community's Response to Climate Change," December 11, 2011. www.cop17-cmp7durban.com/en/news-centre/media-releases/breakthrough-response-to-climate-change-20111211.html.

National and Subnational Efforts, Rather than International Agreements, Are the Best Way to Address Global Warming

Harald Heubaum, as told to Responding to Climate Change

Harald Heubaum is a lecturer in global energy and climate policy at the School of Oriental and African Studies at the University of London. Responding to Climate Change (RTCC) is an organization based in the United Kingdom dedicated to raising awareness about climate change issues and supporting United Nations outreach on this issue.

Replacing the Kyoto Protocol [an international climate change treaty] with a second commitment period is one of the key aims of COP17 [Seventeenth Conference of the Parties to the United Nations Framework Convention on Climate Change (UNFCCC)], which opens in Durban [South Africa] on Monday 28 November [2011].

Since coming into force in 2005 [the Kyoto Protocol] has provided the foundation for global climate talks, but next year [2012] its remit expires.

Opinion is divided over whether we need a second commitment period. The treaty has been derided as ineffective, the USA's refusal to take part has hurt its credibility, while major emitters like India and China are not subject to legally binding targets.

And yet it is the only global treaty we have, and the only agreement that is legally binding.

In part 1 of his analysis of the Kyoto Protocol, Harald Heubaum, Lecturer in Global Energy and Climate Policy at the School of Oriental and African Studies looked back at the treaty's troubled birth and recent history.

It is national and subnational governments rather than international conferences that hold the key to success [in cutting greenhouse gas emissions].

In part 2 [below] he charts a course for the future, asking if Kyoto is not the answer—then what is?

Responding to Climate Change (RTCC): *What should negotiators aim for at COP17?*

Harald Heubaum: International climate change negotiations still suffer from too much of a focus on legally binding targets. Constantly haggling over targets that are not actually enforceable distracts from more important business.

A meaningful outcome at Durban would be for the process as it is to simply stay on track without new targets. Any future round of negotiations should include progress on at least three fronts: increased technology development and transfer, adaptation, as well as a greater acknowledgement that climate change needs to be simultaneously addressed at multiple levels of political authority.

The road to cutting GHG [greenhouse gas] emissions runs through Beijing and New Delhi, Toronto and Sacramento rather than just through Durban or Bonn. That is to say it is national and subnational governments rather than international conferences that hold the key to success.

And yet a bottom-up architecture in which individual countries independently decide by how much to reduce emissions has been criticized as ineffective compared to an inclusive global architecture that sets the targets necessary to hold a rise in global average surface temperatures to 2 degrees Celsius. . . .

Using What Works

What matters is what works. Bottom-up processes have so far produced actual results with renewable portfolio standards, feed-in-tariffs, better fuel efficiency standards, emissions reduction and energy intensity targets and a range of other climate-friendly measures in place at national and subnational levels around the world. The carbon tax just passed by the [Julia] Gillard government in Australia or the levy on coal recently passed by the Indian Parliament are examples of how domestic policy change can have a real impact on pricing carbon and, eventually, reducing CO_2 [carbon dioxide] emissions.

Emissions trading, too, is essentially an example of bottom-up dynamics and certainly of cross-jurisdictional policy learning. The idea did not originate with Kyoto but has its roots in the United States where the 1990 amendments to the Clean Air Act established a highly successful SO_2 [sulfur dioxide] trading scheme. The EU [European Union] and its Member States learned from this experience and early discussions on trading carbon emissions on this side of the Atlantic preceded the Kyoto Protocol. The EU-ETS [European Union Emissions Trading Program] is used to reach Kyoto targets yet it is independent of the treaty.

Should we scrap international efforts in favour of a bottom-up architecture?

We need both. Voicing public and unequivocal support for Kyoto is fine but why should Kyoto II be the only issue on the table? Again, Kyoto failed on emissions targets, credible enforcement mechanisms and inclusiveness. Right now, there is absolutely no indication that a follow-on treaty will fare any better. We should support a continued international process if only to focus attention, keep the issue on the agenda and provide a platform for the exchange of knowledge and best practice. Keeping the Kyoto elements that do work is important but with time running out we now need to use every tool at our disposal—and that includes a bottom-up approach.

The transition to clean energy technologies is, together with improved energy efficiency, the key to reducing global CO_2 emissions.

... which runs the risk of creating a fragmented patchwork system?

Initially, perhaps but there's likely to be greater convergence in the long run. The challenge is to link the approaches in an effective way. However, one of the problems of the UN-led process is that it does not sufficiently appreciate the variety of factors enabling and constraining policy-making at national and subnational levels of political authority.

In contrast, organisations such as GLOBE International have early on worked towards strengthening the role of national legislators and parliaments as crucial to achieving real change. GLOBE has done so in the recognition that one size does not fit all and that individual countries may wish to pursue different avenues towards emissions reductions. The end goal (mitigating climate change) is the same.

Which elements of Kyoto should remain in place?

Technology development and transfer is one example. COP16 [the last climate talks] in Cancun [Mexico] made some progress in designing a new Technology Mechanism but deployment needs to be scaled up and diffusion sped up much more quickly than is currently the case. This requires greatly increased investments into research, development and demonstration (RD&D) as well as a solution to persistent intellectual property rights (IPR) problems.

The transition to clean energy technologies is, together with improved energy efficiency, the key to reducing global CO_2 emissions from electricity and heat generation as well as transport. If renewables cannot do the job alone then this needs to include technologies such as CCS [carbon capture and storage] for natural gas and coal.

What happens if we fail to reduce global carbon emissions to sustainable levels?

We need to get real about the effects of unchecked climate change. At least everyone is now talking about adaptation but it still isn't taken as seriously as it should. Effective mitigation reduces the need to enhance adaptive capacities—the differences between two and six degrees of warming are immense—but it certainly does not make it unnecessary.

There is currently not nearly enough public and private investment in adaptation. As we move deeper into the 21st century this will need to be scaled up considerably. Here again, national governments as well as the UNFCCC are needed to help the private sector overcome investment hurdles.

The UNFCCC's role will likely change over time, from one focused primarily on mitigation to one that puts adaptation at the heart of its efforts. The Adaptation Fund will need to be beefed up and joined up with other programmes such as the Global Environment Facility (GEF), the Green Climate Fund and the UNFCCC's Special Funds (SCCF, LDCF).

The World Should End Fossil Fuel Subsidies to Achieve Emission Reductions

Matthew Yglesias

Matthew Yglesias is a reporter for Slate, *a US-based online magazine of news, politics, and culture.*

What if I told you that we could obtain half the reduction in carbon emissions needed to stave off climate disaster not with new government interventions in the economy but simply by removing existing interventions?

Fatih Birol, chief economist of the International Energy Agency [IEA] is telling you exactly that. In data released this month [January 2012] as part of the IEA's latest World Energy Outlook report, he shows that in 2010 the world spent $409 billion on subsidizing the production and consumption of fossil fuels, dwarfing the word's $66 billion or so of subsidies for renewable energy. Phasing fossil fuel subsidies out would be sufficient to accomplish about half the reduction in greenhouse gas emissions needed to meet the goal of preventing average world temperatures from rising more than 2 degrees Celsius.

You don't hear as much about this as you should largely because the biggest offenders are far from our shores. Still, the scale and scope of the issue is worth dwelling on if only because these subsidies are so wrongheaded.

Far and away the biggest problem seems to be that misguided sense that countries that are large producers of certain kinds of fuels ought to subsidize domestic consumption of the fuel in question. Thus Saudi Arabia spends more than $30 billion a year on gas consumption subsidies while Russia spends $17 billion on natural gas subsidies. Iran, which produces both, subsidizes both, spending $66 billion in total plus an additional $14.4 billion on electricity consumption subsidies. Large-population developing countries such as China, India, and Indonesia are also important players in the subsidy game. In no case do these subsidies make sense.

For starters, the mere fact that your country contains a lot of oil offers no special reason to subsidize gasoline consumption. For one thing, gasoline isn't oil. Like other usable fuels, it needs to be refined from crude. Iran is actually a net importer of refined petroleum products, and the United States has recently become a net exporter of them, even as the situation for crude oil is the reverse. More broadly, the opportunity cost of using a domestically produced barrel of oil is identical to the financial cost of buying a barrel on international markets. In other words, if the Japanese government wants to offer subsidized oil to its citizens, it needs to go buy the oil first from Saudi Arabia. By the same token, if the Saudi government wants to offer subsidized oil to its citizens, it needs to sell less to Japan. The budgetary impact is identical in either case and the merits of the policy have nothing to do with how much oil a country has.

Subsidies Misguided

And what are the merits? Not much. Consumption subsidies are typically justified as beneficial to the poor. But while it's certainly true that in rich countries utility bills and transportation fuel costs disproportionately burden the poor, it's not clear that this is true in the developing world. Here in the United States, only rich people go to fancy restaurants, but everyone needs to run home appliances, which is why higher energy costs hit the poor hardest. In India, however, more than a third of the population doesn't have electricity, and most people don't have cars. China's not as poor as India, but the same logic applies: The people who truly need help are the people who can't afford to take advantage of the subsidies. The IEA calculates that less than 10 percent of global fossil fuel subsidies benefit the poorest 20 percent. These subsidies would be much better spent on a mix of cash grants to the poor, lower taxes to spur growth, and investments in infrastructure and education.

The whole framework of a trade-off between prosperity and sustainability is largely misguided.

But even a direct fuel subsidy for the poor is a pretty bad way to help people. America doesn't go in for lavish spending on fuel consumption subsidies, but we do have something called the Low-Income Home Energy Assistance Program, which offers targeted subsidies to help poor families in cold-weather states to keep their families warm in the winter. This is hardly the worst idea in the world, but you'd do more for the families and the environment if you just gave them cash. Some of that cash might go to pay the heating bill, but some might go to the purchase of sweaters or better insulation, ecologically friendlier solutions that will probably help households more over the long run.

That these kinds of subsidies are misguided counts as conventional wisdom in the economics world, but it's not clear that even economists have recognized the sheer scale of the impact. If roughly half of what needs to be done can be achieved simply by eliminating economic distortions—economic distortions that would be unwise even if there were no concern about pollution—then the whole framework of a trade-off between prosperity and sustainability is largely misguided. The outlook for greener, freer markets gets even brighter when you consider that consumption subsidies aren't the only dirty interventions out there. The U.S. government offers generous tax subsidies for the production of oil and natural gas (each year, President [Barack] Obama proposes to scrap them, and each year Congress declines), and the European Union does the same for coal. Local governments nearly everywhere require the construction of more parking spaces and lower-density buildings than a free market would provide, encouraging excessive driving and energy-intensive large detached homes.

At the end of the day, pure laissez faire can never meet the world's environmental challenges. If you want to reduce greenhouse gas emissions, you need to cap them and then you need to reduce the cap. But a surprisingly large step toward that target can occur by simply allowing the market to do its work by removing the subsidies that encourage lavish and inefficient consumption of fossil fuels.

Efforts to Slow Global Warming Should Focus on Methane and Soot Instead of Carbon Dioxide

R.P. Siegel

R.P. Siegel is an engineer, inventor, and the founder and executive director of Cool Rochester, a nonprofit agency devoted to reducing the carbon footprint of Rochester, New York, by a billion pounds by end of 2012.

Most efforts to slow the impact of global warming have focused on reducing carbon [CO_2] emissions, because, according to the EPA [US Environmental Protection Agency], they are the most dominant and the fastest growing greenhouse gas (GHG). But CO_2 is only one of several greenhouse gases, which also include methane, nitrous oxide, and fluorinated gases, such as hydrofluorocarbons, and soot. A team of scientists led by NASA [National Aeronautics and Space Administration] Goddard's Drew Shindell (who also works at Columbia's Earth Institute), in an article published in this month's [January 2012] issue of *Science*, suggest that an easier and possibly more effective approach, at least in the short term, would be to focus on methane and soot. Why? Because these two pollutants are both fast acting, so reducing their presence in the atmosphere can have a more immediate impact on the overall GHG concentration. If a two degree Celsius increase in average global temperature is seen as the cliff that we are rapidly driving towards, focusing on methane and soot might actually help to slow us down more quickly than our current approach, which focuses on CO_2. Not only that, but according to the paper's title, reducing these two pollutants, could also improve human health and food security.

According to the study, adopting these measures could reduce warming between now and 2050 from 2.2 degrees to 1.3 degrees Celsius.

Dramatically reducing soot levels could save as many as 4.7 million lives each year worldwide.

Starting from the premise that reducing these two pollutants would rapidly mitigate climate risk, the team evaluated roughly 400 emission control measures and found 14 that could reduce either methane or soot in a cost-effective manner, using existing technology.

Many of these, such as banning the burning of agricultural land, capturing methane from landfills and coal mines, fixing leaky pipelines, putting filters on cook stoves and diesel engines, and modifying agriculture practices for rice paddies and manure collection—are already being used effectively in many places.

Not surprisingly, these results were met with an enthusiastic response from people close to the oil industry. It doesn't take a huge leap of imagination to see that they will quickly begin using this analysis as a crowbar to start prying up efforts to reduce CO_2. John D. Graham, who oversaw regulations at the Office of Management and Budget for the George W. Bush administration, said, "This is an important study that deserves serious consideration by policy makers as well as scientists."

Well, it may be, especially considering the health impacts, which would come about as reduced air pollution levels, primarily from soot. Dramatically reducing soot levels could save as many as 4.7 million lives each year worldwide. Two million people die each year, mostly in Africa, from dirty cook stoves.

There could also be agricultural benefits, as soot tends to divert rainfall, causing uneven moisture distribution, flooding and drought. But it is essential to point out at the outset that this does not mean that we should stop trying to reduce CO_2 emissions. That would be a big mistake.

Carbon dioxide is still the No. 1 cause of man-made global warming, accounting for 48 percent of the problem. Soot and methane combined account for 30 percent. They do tend to be shorter acting, though, which means that we will see the results of mitigation sooner. The smart strategy is to focus on both long term and short term impacts. The problem is far too serious for a half-hearted solution.

The results await the response of the broad scientific community. I expect there will be a certain amount of controversy. A number of the scientific studies described in the review by *Skeptical Science* that I covered earlier this week found that aerosols, a category of emissions that includes soot, actually contribute to global *cooling*, by blocking out sunlight and reducing the amount of solar radiation that reaches the Earth. If that's true, then aggressively curtailing it could have some warming effect. Going after methane, however has no apparent downside.

Governments Must Support New Green Energy Technologies More Quickly

Institution of Mechanical Engineers

The Institution of Mechanical Engineers is a London-based professional organization that seeks to provide knowledge and guidance to government, business, and the public on all aspects of mechanical engineering.

The technology needed to cut the world's greenhouse gas emissions by 85% by 2050 already exists, according to a joint statement by eleven of the world's largest engineering organisations.

The statement was presented on Friday 23 September [2011] to the South African Deputy High Commissioner ahead of December's COP17 [Seventeenth Conference of the Parties to the United Nations Framework Convention on Climate Change (UNFCCC)] climate change talks in Durban [South Africa].

The statement says that generating electricity from wind, waves and the sun, growing biofuels sustainably, zero emissions transport, low carbon buildings and energy efficiency technologies have all been demonstrated. However, they are not being developed for wide-scale use fast enough and there is a desperate need for financial and legislative support from governments around the world if they are to fulfil their potential.

Dr Colin Brown, Director of Engineering at the Institution of Mechanical Engineers—one of the eleven organisations supporting the statement—said:

"While the world's politicians have been locked in talks with no output, engineers across the globe have been busy developing technologies that can bring down emissions and help create a more stable future for the planet.

"We are now overdue for government commitment, with ambitious, concrete emissions targets that give the right signals to industry, so they can be rolled out on a global scale."

Items of the Joint Statement

The statement calls for:

- A global commitment at Durban to a peak in greenhouse gas emissions by 2020, followed by substantial reductions by 2050;

- Governments to ensure that green policies do not unfairly and unintentionally act to the detriment of one particular industry or country;

- Intensive effort to train and retrain workforces to ensure we have the right skills for the new industries that will spring up around green technologies;

- A heavier emphasis to be placed on boosting energy efficiency, which is the best available measure to bring down emissions in the short and medium term.

The eleven organisations include the Danish Society of Engineers (IDA), India's Institution of Engineers (IEI), Germany's Association of Engineers (VDI), Australia's Association of Professional Engineers, Scientists and Managers (APESMA) and the UK's Institution of Mechanical Engineers (IMechE). Collectively they represent over 1.2 million engineers spanning four continents.

The joint statement is the product of a landmark biennial conference held yesterday and today [September 22–23, 2011] at the Institution of Mechanical Engineers. The Future Climate 2 conference brought together speakers from government, academia and engineering institutions from around the world to discuss the technologies needed to combat climate change.

The UK Committee for Climate Change ... recommends an energy mix of 40% nuclear, 40% renewable, 15% Carbon Capture and Storage and 5% fossil fuel by 2030.

Highlights from the conference included:

- The German Association of Engineers (VDI) reported that the phasing out of nuclear power in Germany could lead to a doubling in national carbon emissions by 2050, with domestic renewable energy simply unable to fill the gap. To reach a planned 80% reduction in emissions, Germany must brace itself for expensive technological fixes and the large-scale import of green electricity produced by solar power from the Mediterranean;

- The President of the Japanese Society of Mechanical Engineers (JSME) spoke about what happened at the Fukushima nuclear power plant after March's earthquake and tsunami. The 50 year old technology withstood the earthquake but not the tsunami. The Onigawa power plant, far closer to the earthquake's epicentre, survived despite being hit by a 13m high wave because its walls stood 14.8m high. Local villagers even sheltered from the tsunami inside the plant;

- The UK [United Kingdom] Committee for Climate Change, which is advising the Government on its low carbon strategy, recommends an energy mix of 40% nuclear, 40% renewable, 15% Carbon Capture and Storage and 5% fossil fuel by 2030. It also suggests that we should aim for 40% of our vehicles to be hybrid and 20% to be wholly electric by 2030;

- An investigation into the environmental impact of reducing the high level of meat in our diets showed that it would free up tens of thousands of hectares of arable land in the UK. If this land was, in turn, left to revert back to its natural woodland state this could lead to huge reductions in CO_2.

Future Climate 2 Conference

The Future Climate 2 conference took place at the Institution of Mechanical Engineers in London on the 22–23 September 2011. The eleven engineering institutions that signed up to the joint statement were:

- The Institution of Mechanical Engineers (IMechE) (UK)

- The Institution of Engineers (India)

- The Association of German Engineers (VDI) (Germany)

- The Japanese Society of Mechanical Engineers (JSME) (Japan)

- The Association of Professional Engineers, Scientists and Managers (APESMA) (Australia)

- The Danish Society of Engineers (IDA) (Denmark)

- The Civil Engineer Organisation of Honduras (CICH) (Honduras)

- The Swedish Association of Graduate Engineers (Sweden)

- The Norwegian Society of Engineers (NITO) (Norway)

- The Finnish Association of Graduate Engineers (TEK) (Finland)

- The Union of Professional Engineers (UIL) (Finland)

Geoengineering Research Should Be Pursued as a Solution to Global Warming

Dan Vergano

Dan Vergano is a science writer and columnist for USA Today, *a national daily newspaper.*

Scientists call it "geoengineering," but in plain speak, it means things like this: blasting tons of sulfate particles into the sky to reflect sunlight away from Earth; filling the ocean with iron filings to grow plankton that will suck up carbon; even dimming sunlight with space shades.

Each brings its own set of risks, but in a world fretting about the consequences of global warming, are these ideas whose time has come?

With 2010 tying as the world's warmest year on record and efforts to slow greenhouse gas emissions looking stymied, calls are rising for research into engineering our way out of global warming—everything from launching solar shade spacecraft to genetically engineering green deserts. An international consortium of 12 universities and research institutes on Tuesday [February 22, 2011], for example, announced plans to pioneer large-scale "ocean fertilization" experiments aimed at using the sea to pull more greenhouse gases out of the sky.

Once the domain of scientists' off-hours schemes scrawled on cocktail napkins, such geoengineering is getting a serious look in the political realm.

"We're moving into a different kind of world," says environmental economist Scott Barrett of Columbia University.

"Better we turn to asking if 'geoengineering' could work, than waiting until it becomes a necessity."

A National Academy of Sciences' best estimate has global warming bumping up average temperatures by 3 to 7 degrees Fahrenheit by the end of the century. Meanwhile, greenhouse gas emissions that are largely responsible, most from burning the modern economy's main fuels, coal and oil, look set to continue to rise for the next quarter-century, according to Energy Information Agency estimates. "That's where geoengineering comes in," says international relations expert David Victor of the University of California–San Diego. "Research into geoengineering creates another option for the public."

Eruption of Mount Pinatubo

Geoengineering takes its cue from the natural experiment that actually had made the only dent in global warming's rise in the last two decades—the 1991 eruption of Mount Pinatubo in the Philippines, which blasted more than 15 million tons of sulfur dioxide 21 miles high, straight into the stratosphere. The stratosphere suspended those sulfur particles in the air worldwide, where the haze they created scattered and reflected sunlight away from the Earth and cooled global atmospheric temperatures nearly 0.7 to 0.9 degrees Fahrenheit in 1992 and 1993, before finally washing out, according to NASA [National Aeronautics and Space Administration] Goddard Institute for Space Studies estimates. Firing about half that much sulfur into the stratosphere every year for 30 years would help stabilize global warming's rise, National Center for Atmospheric Research climate scientist Tom Wigley estimated in a much-debated 2006 *Science* journal report.

Humanity would effectively become addicted to sky-borne sulfates to keep the cooling on track. The tradeoff is that rain and snow patterns would likely shift, a 2008 Proceedings of the National Academy of Sciences study found, consigning hundreds of millions of the poorest people on the planet in Africa and Asia to recurring drought.

Dumping iron filings into the ocean to spur phytoplankton blooms is the saltwater version of forestation.

"Geoengineering is no longer a taboo topic at scientific meetings. They are looking at it as one more policy prescription," says *Science* magazine reporter Eli Kintisch, author of *Hack the Planet: Science's Best Hope—Or Worst Nightmare—For Averting Climate Catastrophe.* "But it is yet to become a household word." That may be changing, as the terms of debate about geoengineering become clear. On the pro-research side, this October the U.S. House Committee on Science and Technology called for more research into geoengineering "to better understand which technologies or methods, if any, represent viable stopgap strategies for managing our changing climate and which pose unacceptable risks."

On the more cautious side, a United Nations Environment Programme species conservation meeting in Nagoya, Japan, ended that same month with a call for, "no climate-related geoengineering activities," without environmental and scientific review.

What are the actual geoengineering proposals? Broadly, they come in two flavors: those that deal with greenhouse gases directly by soaking up carbon dioxide (the greenhouse gas with the biggest warming impact); and those that seek to limit the sunlight that warms those greenhouse gases. Here's a sampling, from the deep ocean to deep space:

- *Ocean fertilization.* Dumping iron filings into the ocean to spur phytoplankton blooms is the saltwater version of forestation. The increased mass of the plankton's cells would swell with carbon pulled from the air. On the downside, it may kill fish, belch out other greenhouse gases such as methane, and hasn't worked very well in small trials.

- *Forestation.* Intense planting of trees and reclaiming deserts with hardier plants is one of the ideas endorsed at the recent Cancun, Mexico, climate meeting, where representatives of 192 nations made some progress on an international climate agreement. More fantastic versions, endorsed by Princeton physicist Freeman Dyson, would rely on genetic engineering to produce trees that act as natural carbon scrubbers, their trunks swollen with carbon pulled from the air.

- *Cloud engineering.* Painting rooftops white, genetically engineering crops to have shinier surfaces, and floating blocks of white Styrofoam in the oceans are all proposals to mimic the effects of clouds, whose white surfaces reflect sunlight. Pumping sea salt into the sky from thousands of "spray ships" could increase clouds themselves. Cost-effectiveness aside, such cloud-seeding might end up dumping rain on the ocean or already soggy regions, instead of where it's needed.

Sulfur Aerosols

- *Pinatubo a-go-go.* As mentioned above, sulfur aerosols could be fired into the sky by cannons, released by balloons or dropped from planes.

- *Space mirrors.* Hundreds of thousands of thin reflective yard-long disks fired into a gravitational balance point between the sun and Earth could dim sunlight. Cost aside, rocket failures or collisions might lead to a tremendous orbital debris cloud circling the Earth. And a recent *Geophysical Research Letters* space tourism report suggests the rocket fuel burned to launch the needed number of shades would dump enough black soot— which absorbs sunlight and heats the atmosphere—to increase average global temperatures about 1.4 degrees.

"Most of the technologies are not yet proven and are at the theoretical or research phase," an August Congressional Research Service report noted.

Geoengineering technologies, once developed, may enable short-sighted and unwise deployment, with potentially serious unforeseen consequences.

On the environmental side, cutting temperature increases through these techniques may still shift rain and snow patterns, leaving the planet cooler, but it could also trigger droughts across vast swaths of farmland in Africa and India. Further, ocean fertilization could contribute to mass killing of sea life and releases of methane greenhouse gas, while using sulfur aerosols could bring not only drought but also enlarged ozone holes.

Leaving aside the environmental risks each one carries, the estimated costs tend to increase with how quickly each method removes carbon or deflects sunlight. The space reflectors would top the bill at a cost of several trillion dollars over 25 years.

"Geoengineering technologies, once developed, may enable short-sighted and unwise deployment, with potentially serious unforeseen consequences," said a 2009 American Meteorological Society statement. Turning over weather management to human beings raises, "legal, ethical, diplomatic, and even national security concerns," the statement added. Deflected storm tracks could result in floods such as the ones hitting Australia last month [January 2011] or Pakistan last year. And simply cutting temperatures won't stop the rise in ocean acidification arising from increased carbon dioxide levels in the air, which may affect marine life underlying the ocean food web.

Simply putting a worldwide price on carbon emissions from smokestacks and letting the marketplace lead to lower carbon emissions would likely be cheaper and more sensible than geoengineering, says Barrett, the economist. "But let's face it. We're talking about (geoengineering) because we don't have a price on carbon."

That's why geoengineering could happen before a global climate treaty ever passes the U.S. Senate, suggests Victor. International climate talks rest on getting 192 self-interested and short-sighted nations to cooperate in ways that will benefit some and cost others, particularly coal-powered ones such as the United States and China. But with geoengineering, you only need one nation to start "hacking," or geoengineering, the planet.

"It would be not at all surprising to wake up one morning and discover that Chinese testing (of geoengineering) has begun on a large scale," Victor says. "That would freak everyone out and create huge international tensions."

No international treaty governs geoengineering, other than a 2008 amendment to ocean pollution agreements limiting ocean fertilization to research studies.

Still a Foreign Concept to Many

A Yale University survey of 1,001 people nationwide last year found that 1% could correctly describe geoengineering. The field needs to be researched, suggests climate scientist Michael MacCracken of the Climate Institute in Washington, D.C., before opinions harden without accurate information. Geoengineering at this point looks like one of many options in addressing climate change, MacCracken adds, "You can only geoengineer so much before the side effects become so much worse than the cure that it doesn't make sense to bother."

He and others argue geoengineering research should begin in earnest, before some abrupt climate change, such as Greenland's ice sheet melting precipitously, stampedes the world into an overreaction and rush to costly technology as a quick, untested fix.

"No research is really going on in a lot of these areas," he says, raising the prospect of a lot of fruitless or counterproductive climate engineering efforts suddenly sprouting in a global panic about collapsing ice sheets decades from now.

Global warming by itself is a kind of geoengineering, noted as far back as 1896 by the Swedish scientist Svante Arrhenius, who calculated that doubling the amount of carbon dioxide (the most noted greenhouse gas) in the atmosphere by burning fossil fuels would likely warm the atmosphere by 9 degrees. Arrhenius supposed that would take thousands of years to happen, based on fossil fuel use rates at the turn of the century. Instead, the global average temperature has warmed about 1.4 degrees since he made his estimate, as carbon dioxide levels have increased tremendously, and his 9-degree increase is now within the range of forecasts for 2100.

"I think it is settled that some climate engineering research will go forward," Kintisch says. "We haven't seen it enter the national debate yet. Hard to know what will happen when it does. That may be the biggest question."

The World Should Not Waste Resources on Fighting Global Warming

Richard S. Lindzen

Richard S. Lindzen is a professor of meteorology at the Massachusetts Institute of Technology and a global-warming skeptic who writes for various conservative publications.

The notion of a static, unchanging climate is foreign to the history of the earth or any other planet with a fluid envelope. The fact that the developed world went into hysterics over changes in global mean temperature anomaly of a few tenths of a degree will astound future generations. Such hysteria simply represents the scientific illiteracy of much of the public, the susceptibility of the public to the substitution of repetition for truth, and the exploitation of these weaknesses by politicians, environmental promoters, and, after 20 years of media drum beating, many others as well. Climate is always changing. We have had ice ages and warmer periods when alligators were found in Spitzbergen [Norway]. Ice ages have occurred in a hundred thousand year cycle for the last 700 thousand years, and there have been previous periods that appear to have been warmer than the present despite CO_2 [carbon dioxide] levels being lower than they are now. More recently, we have had the medieval warm period and the little ice age. During the latter, alpine glaciers advanced to the chagrin of overrun villages. Since the beginning of the 19th Century these glaciers have been retreating. Frankly, we don't fully understand either the advance or the retreat.

For small changes in climate associated with tenths of a degree, there is no need for any external cause. The earth is never exactly in equilibrium. The motions of the massive oceans where heat is moved between deep layers and the surface provides variability on time scales from years to centuries. Recent work suggests that this variability is enough to account for all climate change since the 19th Century.

A Further Problem

For warming since 1979, there is a further problem. The dominant role of cumulus convection in the tropics requires that temperature approximately follow what is called a moist adiabatic profile. This requires that warming in the tropical upper troposphere be 2–3 times greater than at the surface. Indeed, all models do show this, but the data doesn't and this means that something is wrong with the data. It is well known that above about 2 km altitude, the tropical temperatures are pretty homogeneous in the horizontal so that sampling is not a problem. Below two km (roughly the height of what is referred to as the trade wind inversion), there is much more horizontal variability, and, therefore, there is a profound sampling problem. Under the circumstances, it is reasonable to conclude that the problem resides in the surface data, and that the actual trend at the surface is about 60% too large. Even the claimed trend is larger than what models would have projected but for the inclusion of an arbitrary fudge factor due to aerosol cooling. . . . Inevitably in climate science, when data conflicts with models, a small coterie of scientists can be counted upon to modify the data. Thus, [some scientists] argue that stretching uncertainties in observations and models might marginally eliminate the inconsistency. That the data should always need correcting to agree with models is totally implausible and indicative of a certain corruption within the climate science community.

It turns out that there is a much more fundamental and unambiguous check of the role of feedbacks in enhancing greenhouse warming that also shows that all models are greatly exaggerating climate sensitivity. Here, it must be noted that the greenhouse effect operates by inhibiting the cooling of the climate by reducing net outgoing radiation. However, the contribution of increasing CO_2 alone does not, in fact, lead to much warming (approximately 1 deg. C for each doubling of CO_2).

Even when all models agree, they can all be wrong.

The larger predictions from climate models are due to the fact that, within these models, the more important greenhouse substances, water vapor and clouds, act to greatly amplify whatever CO_2 does. This is referred to as a positive feedback. It means that increases in surface temperature are accompanied by reductions in the net outgoing radiation—thus enhancing the greenhouse warming. All climate models show such changes when forced by observed surface temperatures.

Satellite observations of the earth's radiation budget allow us to determine whether such a reduction does, in fact, accompany increases in surface temperature in nature. As it turns out, the satellite data from the ERBE [Earth Radiation Budget Experiment] instrument shows that the feedback in nature is strongly negative—strongly reducing the direct effect of CO_2 in profound contrast to the model behavior. This analysis makes clear that even when all models agree, they can all be wrong, and that this is the situation for the all important question of climate sensitivity. . . .

According to the UN's Intergovernmental Panel on Climate Change [IPCC], the greenhouse forcing from man made greenhouse gases is already about 86% of what one expects from a doubling of CO_2 (with about half coming from methane, nitrous oxide, freons and ozone), and alarming predictions depend on models for which the sensitivity to a doubling for CO_2 is greater than 2°C, which implies that we should already have seen much more warming than we have seen thus far, even if all the warming we have seen so far were due to man. This contradiction is rendered more acute by the fact that there has been no statistically significant net global warming for the last fourteen years. Modelers defend this situation, as we have already noted, by arguing that aerosols have cancelled much of the warming and that models adequately account for natural unforced internal variability. However, a recent paper points out that aerosols can warm as well as cool, while scientists at the UK's [United Kingdom's] Hadley Centre for Climate Research recently noted that their model did not appropriately deal with natural internal variability thus demolishing the basis for the IPCC's iconic attribution. Interestingly (though not unexpected), the British paper did not stress this. Rather, they speculated that natural internal variability might step aside in 2009, allowing warming to resume. Resume? Thus, the fact that warming has ceased for the past fourteen years is acknowledged. It should be noted that, more recently, German modelers have moved the date for 'resumption' up to 2015.

Nothing About Trends

Climate alarmists respond that some of the hottest years on record have occurred during the past decade. Given that we are in a relatively warm period, this is not surprising, but it says nothing about trends.

Given that the evidence (and I have noted only a few of many pieces of evidence) strongly implies that anthropogenic warming has been greatly exaggerated, the basis for alarm due to such warming is similarly diminished. However, a really important point is that the case for alarm would still be weak even if anthropogenic global warming were significant. Polar bears, arctic summer sea ice, regional droughts and floods, coral bleaching, hurricanes, alpine glaciers, malaria, etc. all depend not on some global average of surface temperature anomaly, but on a huge number of regional variables including temperature, humidity, cloud cover, precipitation, and direction and magnitude of wind. The state of the ocean is also often crucial. Our ability to forecast any of these over periods beyond a few days is minimal (a leading modeler refers to it as essentially guesswork). Yet, each catastrophic forecast depends on each of these being in a specific range. The odds of any specific catastrophe actually occurring are almost zero. This was equally true for earlier forecasts of famine for the 1980's, global cooling in the 1970's, Y2K [computer bug associated with the year 2000] and many others. Regionally, year to year fluctuations in temperature are over four times larger than fluctuations in the global mean. Much of this variation has to be independent of the global mean; otherwise the global mean would vary much more. This is simply to note that factors other than global warming are more important to any specific situation. This is not to say that disasters will not occur; they always have occurred and this will not change in the future. Fighting global warming with symbolic gestures will certainly not change this. However, history tells us that greater wealth and development can profoundly increase our resilience.

Why the Alarm?

In view of the above, one may reasonably ask why there is the current alarm, and, in particular, why the astounding upsurge in alarmism of the past 4 years. When an issue like global warming is around for over twenty years, numerous agendas are developed to exploit the issue. The interests of the environmental movement in acquiring more power, influence, and donations are reasonably clear. So too are the interests of bureaucrats for whom control of CO_2 is a dream-come-true. After all, CO_2 is a product of breathing itself. Politicians can see the possibility of taxation that will be cheerfully accepted because it is necessary for 'saving' the earth. Nations have seen how to exploit this issue in order to gain competitive advantages. But, by now, things have gone much further. The case of ENRON (a now bankrupt Texas energy firm) is illustrative in this respect. Before disintegrating in a pyrotechnic display of unscrupulous manipulation, ENRON had been one of the most intense lobbyists for [the] Kyoto [Protocol]. It had hoped to become a trading firm dealing in carbon emission rights. This was no small hope. These rights are likely to amount to over a trillion dollars, and the commissions will run into many billions. Hedge funds are actively examining the possibilities; so was the late Lehman Brothers. Goldman Sachs has lobbied extensively for the 'cap and trade' bill, and is well positioned to make billions. It is probably no accident that [former vice president and noted environmentalist Al] Gore, himself, is associated with such activities. The sale of indulgences is already in full swing with organizations selling offsets to one's carbon footprint while sometimes acknowledging that the offsets are irrelevant. The possibilities for corruption are immense. Archer Daniels Midland (America's largest agribusiness) has successfully lobbied for ethanol requirements for gasoline, and the resulting demand for ethanol may already be contributing to large increases in corn prices and associated hardship in the developing world (not to mention poorer car performance). And finally, there are the numerous well meaning individuals who have allowed propagandists to convince them that in accepting the alarmist view of anthropogenic climate change, they are displaying intelligence and virtue. For them, their psychic welfare is at stake.

With all this at stake, one can readily suspect that there might be a sense of urgency provoked by the possibility that warming may have ceased and that the case for such warming as was seen being due in significant measure to man, disintegrating. For those committed to the more venal agendas, the need to act soon, before the public appreciates the situation, is real indeed. However, for more serious leaders, the need to courageously resist hysteria is clear. Wasting resources on symbolically fighting ever present climate change is no substitute for prudence. Nor is the assumption that the earth's climate reached a point of perfection in the middle of the twentieth century a sign of intelligence.

Only Immediate Action Will Keep Global Warming Below Dangerous Levels

Richard A. Kerr

Richard A. Kerr is a staff writer for Science, *a journal that provides scientific news, commentary, and cutting-edge research.*

The bad news just got worse: A new study finds that reining in greenhouse gas emissions in time to avert serious changes to Earth's climate will be at best extremely difficult. Current goals for reducing emissions fall far short of what would be needed to keep warming below dangerous levels, the study suggests. To succeed, we would most likely have to reverse the rise in emissions immediately and follow through with steep reductions through the century. Starting later would be far more expensive and require unproven technology.

Published online today [October 23, 2011,] in *Nature Climate Change*, the new study merges model estimates of how much greenhouse gas society might put into the atmosphere by the end of the century with calculations of how climate might respond to those human emissions. Climate scientist Joeri Rogelj of ETH Zurich [a science and technology university in Switzerland] and his colleagues combed the published literature for model simulations that keep global warming below 2°C at the lowest cost. They found 193 examples. Modelers running such optimal-cost simulations tried to include every factor that might influence the amount of greenhouse gases society will produce—including the rate of technological progress in burning fuels efficiently, the amount of fossil fuels available, and the development of renewable fuels. The researchers then fed the full range of emissions from the scenarios into a simple climate model to estimate the odds of avoiding a dangerous warming.

The results suggest challenging times ahead for decision makers hoping to curb the greenhouse [effect]. Strategies that are both plausible and likely to succeed call for emissions to peak this decade and start dropping right away. They should be well into decline by 2020 and far less than half of current emissions by 2050. Only three of the 193 scenarios examined would be *very* likely to keep the warming below the danger level, and all of those require heavy use of energy systems that actually remove greenhouse gases from the atmosphere. That would require, for example, both creating biofuels and storing the carbon dioxide from their combustion in the ground.

"The alarming thing is very few scenarios give the kind of future we want," says climate scientist Neil Edwards of The Open University in Milton Keynes, U.K. [United Kingdom] Both he and Rogelj emphasize the uncertainties inherent in the modeling, especially on the social and technological side, but the message seems clear to Edwards: "What we need is at the cutting edge. We need to be as innovative as we can be in every way." And even then, success is far from guaranteed.

Organizations to Contact

The editors have compiled the following list of organizations concerned with the issues debated in this book. The descriptions are derived from materials provided by the organizations. All have publications or information available for interested readers. The list was compiled on the date of publication of the present volume; names, addresses, phone and fax numbers, and e-mail and Internet addresses may change. Be aware that many organizations take several weeks or longer to respond to inquiries, so allow as much time as possible.

Berkeley Earth Surface Temperature Project(BEST)
Berkeley, CA   94705
(510) 517-9936
e-mail: info@berkeleyearth.org
website: http://berkeleyearth.org

The BEST Project is an effort to do a new analysis of the earth's surface temperature record in a rigorous manner to address criticisms of earlier temperature analyses to determine whether global temperatures are warming and by how much. The study is headed by Richard Muller, a professor of physics at the University of California at Berkeley. Using data from over thirty-nine thousand unique stations, the study so far has found that previous land temperature analyses were accurate, but this does not include ocean temperatures. The project's website provides a wealth of information about the study, its funding, and its conclusions, including a summary of findings, congressional testimony by Richard Muller, and videos.

Center for Climate and Energy Solutions
2101 Wilson Blvd., Ste. 550, Arlington, VA   22201
(703) 516-4146 • fax: (703) 516-9551
website: www.c2es.org

Formerly the Pew Center on Global Climate Change, the Center for Climate and Energy Solutions is an independent, nonpartisan, nonprofit organization working to advance strong policy and action to address the twin challenges of energy and climate change. The center believes that providing safe, reliable, affordable energy while still protecting the global climate is one of the most important challenges of this century. It seeks to provide independent analysis and innovative solutions to address the energy-climate change problem. The center's website is a rich source of information about basic climate science, energy issues, and business impacts. Recent publications available include *Greenhouse Gas Accounting Framework for Carbon Capture and Storage Projects, An Illustrative Framework for a Clean Energy Standard for the Power Sector*, and *Extreme Weather and Climate Change*.

The Climate Reality Project
Palo Alto, CA
website: www.climaterealityproject.org

The Climate Reality Project, formerly known as the Alliance for Climate Protection, is an organization founded and chaired by former vice president Al Gore that seeks to bring the facts about the climate crisis into the mainstream and engage the public in a debate about how to solve it. The group's website is a source for articles about the climate crisis, climate science, and climate solutions and also features a blog and videos from around the world on climate topics. Examples of articles include *Shrinking Glaciers: A Matterhorn Community Responds* and *Doubt Creation*.

Intergovernmental Panel on Climate Change (IPCC)
c/o World Meteorological Organization
7bis Avenue de la Paix, C.P. 2300
Geneva 2 CH-1211
   Switzerland
+41 22 730-8208/84 • fax: +41 22 730-8025/13
e-mail: ipcc-sec@wmo.int
website: www.ipcc.ch

The IPCC is an intergovernmental scientific body set up by the United Nations Environment Programme to provide decision makers and others with an objective source of information about climate change. The IPCC's role is to assess on a comprehensive, objective, open, and transparent basis the latest scientific, technical, and socio-economic literature produced worldwide relevant to the understanding of the risk of human-induced climate change, its observed and projected impacts, and options for adaptation and mitigation. The organization's website provides access to IPCC assessment reports, technical papers, and other publications, including the assessment report *Climate Change 2007*.

National Center for Policy Analysis (NCPA)
601 Pennsylvania Ave. NW, Ste. 900, South Bldg.
Washington, DC   20004
(202) 220-3082
website: www.ncpa.org

The NCPA is a nonprofit, nonpartisan public-policy research organization that promotes private alternatives to government regulation and control and defends the competitive, entrepreneurial private sector. The group takes a skeptical position on global warming. The NCPA's website contains a number of articles under the Environment/Global Warming heading, including, for example, *Reasonable Responses to Climate Change* and *Carbon Offsets: No Sure Bet to Prevent Climate Change*.

Natural Resources Defense Council (NRDC)
40 W. Twentieth St., New York, NY   10011
(212) 727-2700 • fax: (212) 727-1773
e-mail: nrdcinfo@nrdc.org
website: www.nrdc.org

The NRDC is an environmental action organization that uses law, science, and the support of 1.2 million members and online activists to protect the planet's wildlife and wild places and to ensure a safe and healthy environment for all living things. The NRDC website contains a special section on global warming that provides in-depth information about the causes, effects, and solutions for global warming, as well as news articles, factsheets, congressional testimony, blogs, and ideas for how individuals can help reduce their carbon footprint. Representative publications include *An Introduction to Climate Change*, *Climate Scientists Under Siege*, and *Climate Forecast: Thirsty Americans*.

Reason Foundation

1747 Connecticut Ave. NW, Washington, DC   20009
(202) 986-0916 • fax: (202) 315-3623
website: http://reason.org

The Reason Foundation is a national public policy research organization that promotes libertarian principles, including individual liberty, free markets, and the rule of law. The foundation publishes a monthly magazine, *Reason*, and one of its policy areas is climate change. The foundation is skeptical about human-produced climate change, and its website is a source for numerous publications espousing this view. Recent publications include: *Global Warming . . . Cooling . . . or Just Climate Change?* and *How the IPCC Reports Mislead the Public, Exaggerate the Negative Impacts of Climate Change and Ignore the Benefits of Economic Growth*.

Union of Concerned Scientists

2 Brattle Square, Cambridge, MA   02238-9105
(617) 547-5552 • fax: (617) 864-9405
website: www.ucsusa.org

The Union of Concerned Scientists is a leading science-based nonprofit organization working for a healthy environment and a safer world. The group's website contains a special section on global warming with a wealth of information about climate change science and solutions, including articles summarizing the IPCC findings, explanations of various climate change issues, blogs, reports on related topics, and the latest global warming news. Representative publications include *Climate 2030: A National Blueprint for a Clean Energy Economy*, *How to Avoid Dangerous Climate Change*, and *Smoke, Mirrors and Hot Air: How ExxonMobil Uses Big Tobacco's Tactics to Manufacture Uncertainty on Climate Science*.

US Global Change Research Program (USGCRP)
1717 Pennsylvania Ave. NW, Ste. 250, Washington, DC   20006
(202) 223-6262 • fax: (202) 223-3065
website: www.globalchange.gov

The US Global Change Research Program is a federal initiative that coordinates and integrates federal research on changes in the global environment and their implications for society. The USGCRP began as a presidential initiative in 1989 and was mandated by Congress in the Global Change Research Act of 1990 to assist the nation and the world in understanding, assessing, predicting, and responding to human-induced and natural processes of global change. Thirteen federal departments and agencies participate in the USGCRP program, which provides investments for scientific climate change research and observational activities. The USGCRP website is a source of scientific assessment reports, reports to Congress, and other publications about climate change. Recent publications include *Global Climate Change Impacts in the United States (2009)* and *Our Changing Planet: The US Global Change Research Program for Fiscal Year 2011.*

World Wildlife Fund (WWF)
1250 Twenty-Fourth St. NW, Washington, DC
(202) 293-4800
website: www.worldwildlife.org

The WWF is a multinational organization dedicated to conserving and protecting nature. Under the heading "Tackle Climate Change," the WWF website contains a special section on climate change that provides an overview of the issue, details the group's projects in this area, and contains information about what individuals, businesses, and governments can do to help. A search of the WWF website also produces numerous publications on global warming. Examples include *Habitats at Risk: Global Warming and Species Loss in Terrestrial Ecosystems* and *Global Warming and the World's Fisheries: Hot, Hungry, and Gasping for Air.*

Bibliography

Books

David Archer	*Global Warming: Understanding the Forecast.* New York: Wiley, 2011.
Anthony D. Barnosky	*Heatstroke: Nature in an Age of Global Warming.* Washington, DC: Shearwater, 2010.
Heidi Cullen	*The Weather of the Future: Heat Waves, Extreme Storms, and Other Scenes from a Climate-Changed Planet.* New York: HarperCollins, 2010.
Andrew Dessler and Edward A. Parson	*The Science and Politics of Global Climate Change: A Guide to the Debate.* Cambridge: Cambridge University Press, 2010.
Richard Heinberg	*The End of Growth: Adapting to Our New Economic Reality.* Gabriola Island, BC: New Society, 2011.
John Houghton	*Global Warming: The Complete Briefing.* Cambridge: Cambridge University Press, 2009.
Bjørn Lomborg	*Cool It: The Skeptical Environmentalist's Guide to Global Warming.* New York: Vintage, 2010.
Michael E. Mann and Lee R. Kump	*Dire Predictions: Understanding Global Warming—the Illustrated Guide to the Findings of the IPCC.* New York: Dorling Kindersley, 2008.

Edmond A.
Mathez
Climate Change: The Science of Global Warming and Our Energy Future. New York: Columbia University Press, 2009.

Bill McKibben
The Global Warming Reader: A Century of Writing About Climate Change. New York: Penguin, 2012.

Patrick J.
Michaels and
Robert Balling Jr.
Climate of Extremes: Global Warming Science They Don't Want You to Know. Washington, DC: Cato Institute, 2010.

J. Emil Morhardt
Ecological Consequences of Global Climate Change 2011: A Roberts Environmental Center Annual Snapshot. Claremont, CA: Roberts Environmental Center, 2010.

Naomi Oreskes
and Erik M.M.
Conway
Merchants of Doubt: How a Handful of Scientists Obscured the Truth on Issues from Tobacco Smoke to Global Warming. New York: Bloomsbury, 2011.

Charles S.
Pearson
Economics and the Challenge of Global Warming. Cambridge: Cambridge University Press, 2011.

Sherry Seethaler
Damned Lies and Science: How to Sort Through the Noise Around Global Warming, the Latest Health Claims, and Other Scientific Controversies. Upper Saddle River, NJ: FT Press, 2011.

Lawrence Solomon	*The Deniers: The World Renowned Scientists Who Stood Up Against Global Warming Hysteria, Political Persecution, and Fraud (and Those Who Are Too Fearful to Do So).* Minneapolis: Richard Vigilante Books, 2008.
Roy W. Spencer	*The Great Global Warming Blunder: How Mother Nature Fooled the World's Top Climate Scientists.* Jackson, TN: Encounter Books, 2010.
Brian Sussman	*Climategate: A Veteran Meteorologist Exposes the Global Warming Scam.* Washington, DC: WND Books, 2010.
David G. Victor	*Global Warming Gridlock: Creating More Effective Strategies for Protecting the Planet.* Cambridge: Cambridge University Press, 2011.

Periodicals and Internet Sources

Ronald Bailey	"Weathering Man-Made Climate Change," *Reason*, November 22, 2011.
David Biello	"The New Normal? Average Global Temperatures Continue to Rise," *Scientific American*, July 22, 2010.
Jules Boykoff	"Hurricanes, Floods and Wildfires—but Washington Won't Talk Global Warming," *Guardian* (Manchester, UK), September 9, 2011.

Geoff Brumfiel   "Cloud Formation May Be Linked to Cosmic Rays," *Nature*, August 2011.

Charles Q. Choi   "Small Nuclear War Could Reverse Global Warming for Years," National Geographic News, February 22, 2011. http://news.nationalgeographic.com.

Kevin Drum   "Climate Skeptics Take Another Hit," *Mother Jones*, October 21, 2011.

Environment 360   "Opinion Forum: Is Extreme Weather Linked to Global Warming?," June 2, 2011. http://e360.yale.edu.

Mark Follman   "Breitbart Silent About Big Error on His Big Government Site," *Mother Jones*, September 19, 2011.

Andrew Freedman   "Will New Studies Confirming Global Warming Settle Skeptics' Questions? Don't Hold Your Breath," *Washington Post*, October 24, 2011.

Peer Gleick   "Remarkable Editorial Bias on Climate Science at the *Wall Street Journal*," *Forbes*, January 27, 2012.

Lucia Graves   "Global Leaders Call on Canada to Fight Climate Change in New Ad," *Huffington Post*, November 30, 2011. www.huffingtonpost.com.

Charles J. Hanley   "The American 'Allergy' to Global Warming: Why?," *News Tribune*, September 26, 2011. www.newstribune.com.

Richard Harris | "Climate Change: Public Skeptical, Scientists Sure," National Public Radio, June 21, 2011. www.npr.org.

Fiona Harvey | "World Headed for Irreversible Climate Change in Five Years, IEA Warns," *Guardian* (Manchester, UK), November 9, 2011.

Jason Koebler | "Study: Global Warming Is Real," *US News & World Report*, October 21, 2011.

Richared A. Lovett | "Global Warming Silver Lining? Arctic Could Get Cleaner," National Geographic News, September 23, 2011. http://news.nationalgeographic.com.

Alex Morales | "Kyoto Protocol Faces Gap After Emissions Targets End, UN Chief Says," Bloomberg, June 6, 2011. www.bloomberg.com.

James Murray | "Bonn Talks Tackle Post-2012 Carbon Market Fears," BusinessGreen, June 16, 2011. www.businessgreen.com.

Margot Roosevelt | "The Melting Arctic: A Bigger-than-Estimated Impact on Climate," *Greenspace* (blog), *Los Angeles Times*, January 17, 2011. http://latimesblogs.latimes.com.

Quirin Schiermeier | "Increased Flood Risk Linked to Global Warming," *Nature*, February 16, 2011.

Andreas
Schmittner et al.

"Climate Sensitivity Estimated from Temperature Reconstructions of the Last Glacial Maximum," *Science*, November 24, 2011.

Zachary Shahan

"Yes, Global Warming Is Real AND Caused by Humans," Planetsave, October 28, 2011. http://planetsave.com.

James Taylor

"The Death of Global Warming Skepticism, or the Birth of Straw Men?," *Forbes*, October 26, 2011. www.forbes.com.

James Taylor

"New NASA Data Blow Gaping Hole in Global Warming Alarmism," *Forbes*, July 27, 2011. www.forbes.com.

Index

A

Acid rain, 85, 114–115, 117–118
Ad Hoc Working Group, 167, 169
Adaptation Committee, 167, 174
Aerosols
    chlorofluorocarbons from, 19,
        130
    cooling by, 80, 150, 194, 196
    as greenhouse gases, 27, 181
    sulfur aerosols, 189–191
Africa, 137, 149, 165, 188, 190
Agricultural production, 31, 73,
    105, 137–138
Air-conditioning costs, 152, 155
Alaska Conservation Solutions,
    157
Albedo problem, 142–143
Allege, Claude, 71–76
Alley, Richard, 44
American Association for the Ad-
    vancement of Science (AAAS),
    27
American Chemical Society, 28
American Enterprise Institute, 114
American Geophysical Union, 27
American Meteorological Society,
    26–27, 190
American Physical Society (APS),
    27, 71, 93
An Inconvenient Truth (Gore), 87
Antarctica, 64–65, 141, 163
Anthropogenic global warming
    (AGW) hypothesis
    climate change vs., 30
    Gore, Al, theory of, 61

ideology vs. science, 108–112,
    128–130
overview, 126–128
rejection of, 62–63
support for, 41, 101, 126
Anti-global-warming efforts, 20
Arctic sea ice melt, 24, 25, 156
Arrhenius, Svante, 18, 45, 192
Asia, 138, 164, 188
    See also China; Japan
Association of Professional Engi-
    neers, Geologists, and Geophysi-
    cists of Alberta (APEGGA), 94
Association of Professional Engi-
    neers, Scientists and Managers
    (APESMA), 185
Atmospheric temperatures, 50, 52,
    61, 64, 187
Australia, 172, 190
Australia's Association of Profes-
    sional Engineers, 183
Australia's Climate Commission,
    127

B

Bali Climate Declaration by Lead-
    ing Scientists, 103–105
Barrett, Scott, 186–187, 191
Benedict XVI (Pope), 127
Berger, Eric, 46
Bergeron, Louis, 144–147
Berkeley Earth Surface Tempera-
    ture (BEST) Project
    concessions over, 49–51
    establishment of, 69–70

global warming has stopped,
54–59
global warming predictions
from, 38–39, 94–95, 101, 108
human contribution factors,
48–53
natural causes of global
warming, 51–53
no new data from, 48–49
overview, 48
peer review process of, 58–59
temperature rise and, 109–111
Berkeley University, 54
Big Bang theory, 33
Birol, Fatih, 102, 175
Blizzards, 132–133
Bolin, Bert, 81
Boreal forest changes, 158
Bottom-up processes, 171–172
Brazil, 19, 97, 145, 150
Brennan, E. Jean, 156–161
Brown, Colin, 182–183
Brown, Lester, 148
Bush, George H.W., 118
Bush, George W., 180

C

Calder, Nigel, 81
Canada, 121, 144, 158, 164, 169
Cap-and-Trade Bill, 62–63, 198
Capital Institute, 124
Carbon Capture and Storage
(CCS), 174, 184
Carbon dioxide emissions
atmospheric concentrations
of, 43–45
as climate regulators, 44
from coal, 18
danger of, 72
from fossil fuels, 90

global warming exaggerations
over, 100, 105
growth patterns of, 51, 53
impact of, 124, 150
increase in, 12, 124–125, 195
nature of, 72–73
ocean chemistry impact by,
160
reduction of, 20, 175–178,
179–181
regulation of, 82–83, 190,
197–198
unethical claims over, 95
Carbon tax, 172
Cardiovascular problems, 154
Carrington, Damian, 148–151
Catholic Church, 127
Cato Institute, 114
Central America, 160
CERN study. *See* European Organization for Nuclear Research
Challenger disaster, 129
Charles G. Koch Foundation, 70
Charney Report, 46
Chevron oil, 123
China, 21, 145, 167–168, 176–177
Chlorofluorocarbons (CFCs), 19,
130
Civil Engineer Organisation of
Honduras (CICH), 185
Clean Air Act, 96, 172
Climate change
as already happening, 136–139
concerns overstated over, 93
debate over, 18
doubts over, 28, 33, 64
future trends, 138–139
human effect on, 119
impact of, 121–122, 138
IPCC report, 19–20, 23–25

scientific understanding of, 28–29

snow and ice decreases, 140–143

See also Global warming; Greenhouse gas (GHG) emissions

Climate Research journal, 104

Climategate Scandal, 61, 69, 110

Climatic Research Unit (CRU), 55, 57, 61, 68–69

Clouds

changes to, 46, 53

cosmic ray impact on, 40–41

cumulus convection of, 194

engineering of, 189

global warming impact on, 65, 79

influence of, 56, 72, 80, 195

seeding of, 60, 80

See also Cosmics Leaving Outdoor Droplets (CLOUD) study

Coal

Australian levy on, 172

banning of, 180

burning of, 18, 23, 44, 124, 152, 187

carbon capture and storage for, 174

energy from, 48

government subsidies for, 178

mining for, 63

reliance on, 191

Cohen, Roger, 101

Cold War, 115, 116

Columbia University, 146, 148, 186

Compact fluorescent light (CFL) bulbs, 155

Competitive Enterprise Institute (CEI), 113, 115

Conway, Erik M., 113–120

Cooler Heads Coalition, 113

COP17. *See* Seventeenth Conference of the Parties to the United Nations Framework Convention on Climate Change (UNFCCC)

Coral reef bleaching events, 159–160

Corn belt, 145

Cosmic rays

hypothesis of, 81

impact on climate, 40–42, 52–53

temperature control and, 60

Cosmics Leaving Outdoor Droplets (CLOUD) study

cloud effects on global warming, 56, 91–92

impact of cosmic rays, 40

temperature fluctuations and, 80, 81–82

Costa Rica, 160

Costa-Roberts, Justin, 147

Crop models, 144–145

Crutzen, Paul, 130

Cryosphere, 140

Cumulus convection of clouds, 194

Curry, Judith, 55–59, 95

D

Daniels Midland (agribusiness), 198

Danish Society of Engineers (IDA), 183, 185

Danish Space Research Institute, 81

Darwin, Charles, 33
David, Laurie, 87
de Freitas, Chris, 73, 104
Deforestation, 31, 34, 152, 168
Dengue fever, 153
Department of Earth and Atmospheric Sciences, 55
Dessler, Andrew, 47
Disaster relief activities, 165
The Discovery of Global Warming (Weart), 45
Donohue, Thomas, 124
Doran, Peter T., 29
Droughts
    as climate change measure, 122
    crops to tolerate, 147
    disaster relief efforts and, 165
    increase of, 24, 134–135, 152, 156
    recurring nature of, 188
    risk from, 103, 153
    soot impact on, 181
    temperature impact on, 190, 196
Durban Platform, 167–169, 183
Dust Bowl phenomenon, 105, 134

E

Earth Policy Institute, 148
Earth Radiation Budget Experiment (ERBE), 195
Earth Summit, 19–20
Earth system science, 144
Earth Systems Science Center, 52
East Anglia University, 55, 57, 68
The Economist (newspaper), 54, 56
Edwards, Niel, 201
Einstein, Albert, 33, 78

Electric vehicles, 184
Energy Information Agency, 187
ENRON company, 198
ETH Zurich university, 200
Ethanol for gasoline, 198
European Organization for Nuclear Research (CERN)
    climate model findings by, 80
    on cosmic rays, 52
    human-caused global warming, 40–42
    nature-caused global warming, 60–63
    overview, 60–61
    solar theory tests by, 92
    See also Cosmics Leaving Outdoor Droplets (CLOUD) study
European Union, 168, 172, 178
European Union Emissions Trading Program (EU-ETS), 172
Everett, John, 96–97
ExxonMobil, 20, 101, 123, 125

F

Farmers and global warming
    agricultural production, 31, 73, 105, 137–138
    global food prices, 148–151
    impact of, 144–147
    rain-fed agriculture, 137–138
    rice production, 145
    US production impact, 150–151
    wheat production, 144–145
Ferrara, Peter, 48–53
Financial Post (newspaper), 41, 81, 92
Finnish Association of Graduate Engineers (TEK), 185

Flanner, Mark, 142–143

Flooding
damage from, 149
global warming impact on, 153, 196–197
from hurricanes, 135
increase in, 24, 132, 134–135, 138
inland flash flooding, 137
risk from, 103
soot impact on, 181

Food prices and global warming, 148–151

Forestation experiments, 188, 189

Fossil fuel industry
climate change denial by, 122–124
ending subsidies to, 175–178
funding global-warming denial by, 121–125
overview, 121–122

Fossil fuels
cutting back on, 21, 24, 98, 155
danger of, 91
global warming and, 18, 34, 90

France, 145

Freedman, Andrew, 43–47

Freedom of Information laws, 86

Fukushima nuclear power plant disaster, 184

Future Climate 2 conference, 183–184, 185

G

Galileo, Galilei, 33

Gelbspan, Ross, 123

Genetically engineering green deserts, 186

Geoengineering research
as foreign concept, 191–192
Mount Pinatubo eruption, 187–189
overview, 186–187
as solution to global warming, 186–192
sulfur aerosols, 189–191

Geological Sciences at the University of Strathclyde, 77

Geological Society of America (GSA), 28

Geophysical Research Letters report, 189

George C. Marshall Institute, 101, 114, 116–119

Georgia Institute of Technology, 55

German Association of Engineers (VDI), 183, 184, 185

Giaever, Ivar, 71–74, 93–95

Gillard, Julia, 172

Gingrich, Newt, 122

Glacier melt
fluxuations in, 18, 193
fossil fuel impact on, 116
from global warming, 24, 27, 136, 156, 160, 197

Gleick, Peter, 32–35, 99

Global Climate Coalition, 119

Global cooling, 19, 50, 85, 181, 197

Global Environment Facility (GEF), 174

Global warming
Albedo problem, 142–143
effects of, 153–155
food price increase from, 148–151
media coverage of, 20

natural causes of, 51–53
overview, 18–21, 132–135
research fraud over, 61–63
resources should not be wasted on, 193–199
security challenges for military from, 162–165
snow and ice decreases, 140–143
See also Anthropogenic global warming (AGW) hypothesis; Climate change; Health concerns; Temperature cycles; Wildlife threat

Global warming, actions to address
geoengineering research, 186–192
green energy technology support, 182–185
immediate need for, 200–201
impact of trends on, 196–197
national and subnational efforts, 170–174
overview, 167–169, 193–194
reduction of methane and soot, 179–181
See also Kyoto Protocol

Global warming, is not scientifically proven
BEST study shows stoppage of, 54–59
carbon dioxide impact, 77–79
critical review needed over, 75–76
human contribution not addressed, 48–53
hypocrisy over, 87–88
nature controls Earth's temperatures, 60–63
no proof of apocalyptic event, 64–66

politics and belief over, 79–82
research fraud with, 61–63
science is new and untested, 84–89

Global warming, is scientifically proven
BEST Project study on, 38–39
CERN study and, 40–42
conclusions compelling, 32–35
debate over, 36–39
human causes, 26–31
immediate action needed against, 34–35
overview, 23–25, 26–28
peer-reviewed journals on, 29–30
research on danger of, 43–47
sign-on statements, 30–31

Global warming, skepticism
attempts to undermine evidence, 113–120
by conservative Republicans, 126–130
debate over, 90–98
denial over, 118–120
ideology vs. science, 108–112, 128–130
out-of-date research on, 99–107
over science of climatology, 84–85
overview, 68–70, 90–92, 99–101
scientists question, 71–76
solid science needed, 97–98
unethical claims over, 95–97
as working hypothesis, 77–83

Global Warming Policy Foundation, 56

Global Warming Solutions Act (2006), 97

GLOBE International, 173

Goddard Institute for Space Studies (GISS), 68, 109–110, 187
Gore, Al, 61, 86–87
Graham, John D., 180
Grantham Institute for Climate Change and the Environment, 111
Green Climate Fund, 167, 174
Green energy technologies, 182–185
Greenhouse effect, 18, 19, 152
Greenhouse gas (GHG) emissions
    amplifying effect of, 195
    atmospheric removal of, 201
    chlorofluorocarbons, 19, 130
    as climate regulators, 44
    dangerous levels of, 200–201
    as global warming cause, 116
    growth patterns of, 51
    hydrofluorocarbons, 152, 179
    increase in, 23, 28, 45, 187
    justifying policies against, 74
    key to cutting, 171
    methane gas, 19, 24, 179–181, 190
    nitrous oxide, 44, 152, 179, 195
    perfluorocarbons, 152
    reduction of, 24–25, 31, 71 168
    stabilization of, 20–21
    temperature fluxuations, 37
    See also Aerosols; Carbon dioxide emissions
Greenland, 65, 163, 191
Gross domestic product (GDP), 62
Groundhog Day blizzard, 132
The Guardian (newspaper), 54
Guelph University, 57

H

Hack the Planet: Science's Best Hope—Or Worst Nightmare—For Averting Climate Catastrophe (Kintisch), 188
Hadley Centre for Climate Prediction and Research, 68, 196
Hansen, James, 118
Hanta virus, 153
Happer, William, 101
Harvard Medical School, 153
Health concerns
    from global warming, 152–155
    overview, 152–155
    steps to control, 155
    threat to, 153–155
Heartland Institute, 51–53, 70, 114
Heat stroke, 153, 154–155
Heat waves, 24, 103, 132, 137, 149, 153–154
Heinz Center, 160
Heritage Foundation, 62
Heubaum, Harald, 170–174
Historical Climatology Network (DOE), 36
Holdren, John, 101
Hurricanes
    detection equipment for, 37–38
    flooding from, 135
    global warming link, 36, 91
    increase in, 24, 37
    Hurricane Irene, 135
Hybrid vehicles, 184
Hydrofluorocarbons (HFCs), 152, 179
Hydrologic cycle alterations, 34

I

Ice ages, 18, 23, 43–45, 51, 193
Ideology vs. science in global
   warming, 108–112, 128–130
The Independent (newspaper), 54
India
   energy consumption, 176–177
   fossil fuel subsidies, 176
   global warming exaggerations,
      93
   greenhouse gas emissions in,
      21, 168
   Kyoto Protocol and, 170
   reducing greenhouse emis-
      sions, 183
   wheat production drops, 145
Inhofe, James, 96, 113
Inland flash flooding, 137
Institute for Scientific Information
   (ISI), 29
Institution of Engineers (IEI), 183,
   185
Institution of Mechanical Engineers (IMechE), 182–185
Intellectual property rights (IPR),
   173
Intergovernmental Panel on Climate Change (IPCC)
   carbon dioxide impact studies,
      72
   climate change report, 19–20,
      23–25, 30, 100
   climate impact, 136–139, 163
   on climate sensitivity, 46
   cosmic ray hypothesis, 81
   function of, 23
   greenhouse forcing, 195
   health impact of climate
      change, 153

human effect on climate
   change, 119
inflated climate forecasts of,
   74
mistakes by, 33
as origin of global warming
   scare, 95–97
temperature estimates by, 36,
   39, 50, 146
International Energy Agency
   (IEA), 102, 106, 175
Iran, 176
Hurricane Irene, 135
Italy, 150

J

Japan, 20, 37, 169, 176, 188
Japanese Society of Mechanical
   Engineers (JSME), 184, 185
Jastrow, Robert, 116
Jenkins, David, 129
Jones, Phil, 68
Journal of Geophysical Research, 58
Juday, Glenn, 157, 158

K

Kauppinen, Jyrki, 60
Kennicutt, Mahlon, II, 162–165
Kerr, Richard A., 200–201
Keystone pipeline, 91
Keyworth, George, 117
Kidney stones, 153
Kintisch, Eli, 188, 192
Kirkby, Jasper, 41, 81–82
Kyoto Protocol
   ENRON support of, 198
   extension of, 167–168
   failure of, 20–21

pollution concerns under, 88
renewal considerations, 170–173

L

La Niña phenomenon, 134
Large Hadron Collider, 60
Law of the Sea Treaty, 164
Lawrence Livermore National Laboratory, 119
Likens, Gene, 118
Lindzen, Richard S., 98, 101, 193–199
Little Ice Age, 51
Lobell, David, 144, 146–147
Lovejoy, Tom, 160
Low-Income Home Energy Assistance Program, 177
Lysenko, Trofim, 73, 74

M

MacCracken, Michael, 191–192
The Mail on Sunday (newspaper), 54–55
Malaria, 153
Malnutrition concerns, 153
Massachusetts Institute of Technology (MIT), 98
Masters, Jeff, 121
McCarthy, Joseph, 34–35
McGill University, 146
McKibben, Bill, 121–125
McKittrick, Ross, 57, 58–59
McQuillan, Karin, 90–98
Meat diet concerns, 185
Media coverage of global warming, 20

Met Office and Climatic Research Unit, 37, 49
Methane gas, 19, 24, 179–181, 190
Mexico, 144–145, 150, 173, 189
Michaels, Patrick, 64–66, 104
Middle East, 149
Moist adiabatic profile, 194
Montreal Protocol, 19
Mount Pinatubo eruption, 187–189
Muller, Elizabeth, 110–111
Muller, Richard A.
    Climategate emails, 69
    global warming debate, 36–39
    human cause of global warming, 112
    land temperature data, 49–51, 94–95
    See also Berkeley Earth Surface Temperature (BEST) Project
Murdoch, Rupert, 99, 105, 107

N

National Academy of Sciences
    Charney Report by, 46
    climate change report by, 28–29, 126
    computer weather prediction accuracy, 94
    global warming conclusions and, 32–35, 99–100, 104, 116
    importance of science, 30–31
    sulfur in stratosphere, 187–188
    temperature data, 187
National Aeronautics and Space Administration (NASA)
    accusations of falsifying research, 113

climate change impact, 136–139

climate change studies by, 109

Earth photograph by, 121

focus on methane and soot, 179

Mount Pinatubo eruption, 187

solar activity and global warming, 118

temperature data from, 52, 68

temperature stations by, 49

National Center for Atmospheric Research (NCAR), 68, 106, 187

National Oceanic and Atmospheric Administration (NOAA), 37, 49, 68, 96, 132

National Research Council of the National Academies, 29, 162

National Security Implications of Climate Change for US Naval Forces report, 162

National Snow and Ice Data Center, 141

Nature (magazine), 58, 80, 92

Nature Climate Change (magazine), 200

Nature Geoscience (journal), 140

Nature Journal of Science, 60–63

The New Scientist (magazine), 81

New York Times (newspaper), 48

Newton's laws, 78

Nierenberg, William, 116–117

Nitrous oxide, 44, 152, 179, 195

Nordhaus, William, 74

Norwegian Society of Engineers (NITO), 185

O

Obama, Barack, 71, 90–91, 93, 178

Ocean fertilization experiments, 186, 188

Ocean ice melt, 64

Ocean passage in Arctic, 164–165

Ocean temperatures, 57, 64–66

Office of Management and Budget, 180

Oil and gas development, 91, 97–98

The Open University, 201

Oregon State University, 43

Oreskes, Naomi, 29, 113–120, 123

Ozone depletion, 19, 114, 119, 154

P

Pacific Decadal Oscillation (PDO), 51

Pakistan, 190

Pasteur, Louis, 33

Penn State University, 44

Perfluorocarbons (PFCs), 152

Perlmutter, Saul, 109

Perovich, Don, 142–143

Perry, Rick, 111

Peterson, Charles, 159

Plait, Phil, 108–112

Polar bear threat, 157–158

Pollution concerns, 88, 153–154

Pontifical Academy of Sciences, 127

Prehistoric climate variations, 18

Q

Qatar, 168

Quadrennial Defense Review, 126

R

Rain-fed agriculture, 137–138
Randall, Keith, 162–165
Ravi, Thilaka, 152–155
Reagan, Ronald, 116, 117–118
Recycling efforts, 155
Refrigeration costs, 19, 152
Republicans for Environmental
  Protection, 130
Republicans' skepticism over glo-
  bal warming, 126–130
Research, development and dem-
  onstration (RD&D), 173
Respiratory problems, 154
Responding to Climate Change
  (RTCC), 170–174
Rice production, 145
R.J. Reynolds Tobacco, 115
Rockefeller Foundation, 147
Rockefeller University, 94
Rogelj, Joeri, 200
Rohde, Robert, 38
Romm, Joe, 99–107
Romney, Mitt, 122
Root, Terry, 161
Rose, David, 54–59
The Royal Society, 92–93
Russia, 145, 150, 169, 176

S

Salt marsh habitats, 157
Santer, Benjamin, 119
Santorum, Rick, 122
Saudi Arabia, 176
Sayet, Evan, 84–89
Schlenker, Wolfram, 146–147, 148,
  150
Schmitt, Harrison H., 101

Schmittner, Andreas, 43–44
Schwarzenegger, Arnold, 114
Science (magazine)
  climate change impact studies,
    146
  climate change scenarios, 43,
    58
  doubt over reporting accu-
    racy, 47, 100
  focus on methane and soot,
    179
  sulfur in stratosphere, 187–
    188
  temperatures and crop yields,
    149
Science Express (magazine), 145
SciGuy blog, 46
Sea-ice loss, 158, 164
Sea-level rise, 31, 34, 137, 156, 163
Security challenges for military,
  162–165
Seitz, Frederick, 115–116
Serreze, Mark, 141
Seventeenth Conference of the
  Parties to the United Nations
  Framework Convention on Cli-
  mate Change (UNFCCC), 170,
  182
Shindell, Drew, 179
Siegel, R.P., 179–181
Sierra snowpack reduction, 31
Simpson, Joanne, 94
Singer, S. Fred, 51, 94, 117, 118,
  119
Skeptical Science (website), 46,
  181
Smoking and global warming,
  114–115
Snow and ice decreases, 140–143

Solar activity, 51, 56, 64, 118
  See also cosmic rays
Solar heater use, 155
Solar shade spacecraft, 186
Solomon, Lawrence, 41, 81, 92
Soot emissions, 179–181
South Africa, 54
Soviet Union, 73, 116
Soybean production, 145
Space mirrors, 189
Spencer, Roy, 52
Spogli Institute for International
  Studies, 147
Spotts, Pete, 140–143
Stafford, Michael, 126–130
Stanford University, 144, 147, 161
Stern, Nicholas, 25, 120
Strategic Defense Initiative (SDI),
  116
Strategic Planning and Programs
  ExxonMobil Corporation, 101
Street, Chriss W., 60–63
Sulfur aerosols, 189–191
Sulfur hexafluoride (SF6), 152
Sun spot cycles, 51
Surface temperature, 26, 38, 43
  See also Berkeley Earth Sur-
    face Temperature (BEST)
    Project
Swedish Association of Graduate
  Engineers, 185

T

Temperature cycles
  atmospheric, 50, 52, 61, 64,
    187
  crop yields and, 149
  as declining, 68
  estimates of, 146

geoengineering to impact, 190
historical periods of, 92, 144
impact on corn belt, 145
impact on ozone layer, 154
influence of, 56
nature controls, 60–63
ocean temperatures, 57
rise in, 108, 187
surface temperature, 26, 38,
  43
Terra satellite data, 52
Texas A&M University, 46–47, 162
Tornadoes, 36, 38, 132–134
Tree ring data, 68
Trenberth, Kevin, 72, 100, 102
Tropical rain forest loss, 137
Tropical Storm Lee, 135
Tucker, D.R., 126, 129
Tufte, Edward, 129

U

UK Committee for Climate
  Change, 184
Union of Concerned Scientists,
  26–31, 101
Union of Professional Engineers
  (UIL), 185
United Kingdom (UK), 81
United Nations (UN), 19, 23,
  95–97
United Nations Climate Change
  Conference, 169n1
United Nations Environment Pro-
  gramme, 188
United Nations Food and Agricul-
  ture Organization, 146
United Nations Framework Con-
  vention on Climate Change
  (UNFCCC), 20, 174

University of Alabama, 52
University of Alaska, 157
University of California, 69, 187
University of Delaware, 146
University of Michigan, 142
University of North Carolina, 159
University of Pennsylvania, 69
University of Wisconsin, 146
Urban-heating bias, 39, 50
US Army Corps of Engineers Cold Regions Research and Engineering Laboratory, 142
US Climate Change Research Program, 29
US Committee on Science and Technology, 188
US Department of Energy, 36
US Environmental Protection Agency (EPA), 69, 70n1, 96, 179
US Weather Satellite Service, 94

V

Vasey, Gary M., 77–83
Vehicle emissions, 24
Vergano, Dan, 186–192
Victor, David, 187, 191

W

Walker Institute for Climate System Research, 149
Wall Street Journal (newspaper)
   Climategate Scandal, 61
   global warming denial by, 99–100, 107, 122–123
   reporting on research irregularities, 119
   temperature records, 49

Ward, Bob, 111
Washington Post (newspaper), 48, 51, 54, 95
Water supply concerns, 31, 34, 98, 137
Water vapor, 19, 152, 159
Watts, Anthony, 36, 49, 110
Weart, Spencer, 45
Wheat production, 144–145
Wheeler, Tim, 149
Wigley, Tom, 68, 187
Wildfires, 132, 135, 149, 157
Wildlife threat, from global warming
   arctic and boreal impact, 157–158
   marine and coastal impact, 159–161
   overview, 156–157
   population decline, 161
Williams, Deborah, 157
Woods Institute for the Environment, 147
Wordsworth, William, 61
World Day of Peace, 127
World Energy Outlook (WEO), 106, 175
World Meteorological Association, 68
Wright, Glenn, 40–42

Y

Yglesias, Matthew, 175–178

Z

Zero emissions transport, 182
Zimmerman, Maggie Kendall, 29

CPSIA information can be obtained
at www.ICGtesting.com
Printed in the USA
FFOW031423040213
825FF